Contents

Caramel Apple Cake

Total Time Taken: 1 ½ hours
Yield: 12 Servings
Ingredients:
Cake:

- ½ cup applesauce
- ½ teaspoon cinnamon powder
- ½ teaspoon ground ginger
- ½ teaspoon salt
- 1 ¼ cups white sugar
- 1 cup butter, softened
- 1 teaspoon baking soda
- 2 cups all-purpose flour
- 2 red apples, cored and diced
- 4 eggs

Glaze:

- ¼ teaspoon salt
- ½ cup heavy cream
- 1 cup white sugar

Directions:

1. For the cake, combine the sugar, butter and eggs in a container until creamy.
2. Stir in the applesauce then put in the flour, baking soda, salt and cinnamon, as well as ginger and apples.
3. Spoon the batter in a 9-inch round cake pan coated with baking paper.
4. Pre-heat the oven and bake at 350F for about forty-five minutes.
5. Let the cake cool in the pan then move to a platter.
6. For the glaze, melt the sugar in a heavy saucepan until it sppears amber in colour.
7. Put in the cream and salt and stir until melted and smooth.
8. let the glaze cool in the pan then sprinkle it over the cake.

Nutritional Content of One Serving:
Calories: 411 Fat: 18.9g Protein: 4.4g Carbohydrates: 59.1g

Caramel Banana Cake

Total Time Taken: 1 hour
Yield: 12 Servings
Ingredients:

- ¼ cup dark brown sugar
- ½ cup caramel sauce
- ½ teaspoon ground cardamom
- ½ teaspoon salt

- ¾ cup butter, softened
- 1 cup buttermilk
- 1 cup white sugar
- 1 teaspoon cinnamon powder
- 2 cups all-purpose flour
- 2 ripe bananas, mashed
- 2 teaspoons baking powder
- 4 eggs

Directions:
1. Mix the butter with sugars for five minutes until creamy. Put in the eggs, one at a time, then mix in the bananas.
2. Fold in the flour, spices, baking powder and salt, alternating it with buttermilk.
3. Pour the batter in a 9-inch round cake pan.
4. Sprinkle the batter with caramel sauce and preheat your oven and bake the cake at 350F for about forty-five minutes or until a toothpick inserted in the center comes out clean.
5. Let the cake cool in the pan and serve, sliced.

Nutritional Content of One Serving:
Calories: 334 Fat: 13.4g Protein: 5.2g Carbohydrates: 50.6g

Caramel Pineapple Upside Down Cake

Total Time Taken: 1 ½ hours
Yield: 14 Servings

Ingredients:
- ¼ cup whole milk
- ¼ teaspoon salt
- ½ cup butter, softened
- ½ cup canola oil
- ½ cup cornstarch
- ½ cup light brown sugar
- ½ cup white sugar
- 1 cup all-purpose flour
- 1 cup shredded coconut
- 1 teaspoon baking soda
- 2 tablespoons butter
- 3 eggs
- 6 slices pineapple

Directions:
1. Melt the white sugar in a saucepan until it sppears amber in colour.
2. Sprinkle the melted sugar on the bottom of a 9-inch round cake pan coated with baking paper.
3. Top the caramelized sugar with butter and set aside for later.
4. For the batter, combine the butter, oil and brown sugar until fluffy and creamy.

5. Fold in the eggs and milk then put in the remaining ingredients and mix using a spatula.
6. Spoon the batter over the pineapple slices and preheat your oven and bake at 350F for about forty minutes or until a toothpick inserted in the center comes out clean.
7. Let the cake cool in the pan for about ten minutes then flip it over on a platter.
8. Serve chilled.

Nutritional Content of One Serving:
Calories: 309 Fat: 19.2g Protein: 2.9g Carbohydrates: 33.6g

Caramel Pumpkin Cake

Total Time Taken: 1 ½ hours
Yield: 12 Servings
Ingredients:

Cake:

- ¼ cup white sugar
- ¼ cup whole milk
- ½ cup coconut oil, melted
- 1 cup dark brown sugar
- 1 cup pumpkin puree
- 1 pinch salt
- 1 teaspoon baking powder
- 1 teaspoon baking soda
- 1 teaspoon cinnamon powder
- 1 teaspoon ground ginger
- 2 cups all-purpose flour
- 4 eggs

Caramel frosting:

1. 1 cup butter, softened
2. 2 cups powdered sugar
3. 1 pinch salt
4. ½ cup caramel sauce

Directions:

1. For the cake, combine the flour, baking powder, baking soda, spices and salt in a container.
2. In a separate container, mix the coconut oil, pumpkin puree, eggs, sugars and milk.
3. Pour this mixture over the dry ingredients and mix thoroughly.
4. Pour the batter in 2 circular cake pans coated with baking paper.
5. Preheat your oven and bake the cake at 350F for 35 minutes or until it rises completely and is aromatic.
6. Let the cakes cool in the pans then level them and set aside for later.
7. For the frosting, combine the butter, sugar and salt in a container for about five to seven minutes or until twofold in volume and firm.
8. Stir in the caramel sauce.
9. Use half of the frosting to fill the cake and the half that is left over to garnish the cake.

10. Serve fresh.

Nutritional Content of One Serving:
Calories: 495 Fat: 26.4g Protein: 4.8g Carbohydrates: 63.2g

Caramel Spice Cake

Total Time Taken: 1 ¼ hours
Yield: 8 Servings
Ingredients:
Cake:
- ¼ teaspoon ground nutmeg
- ½ cup butter, softened
- ½ cup sour cream
- ½ teaspoon ground cardamom
- ½ teaspoon ground ginger
- ¾ cup light brown sugar
- 1 1/4 cups all-purpose flour
- 1 teaspoon baking soda
- 1 teaspoon cinnamon powder
- 3 eggs

Glaze:
- ½ cup heavy cream
- ½ teaspoon salt
- 1 cup white sugar

Directions:
1. For the cake, sift the flour, baking soda, spices and salt in a container.
2. In a separate container, combine the butter and sugar until creamy. Stir in the eggs and mix thoroughly then put in the sour cream and mix thoroughly.
3. Fold in the flour mixture then pour the batter in a 9-inch round cake pan covered with parchment paper.
4. Pre-heat the oven and bake at 350F for around forty minutes or until a toothpick inserted in the center comes out clean.
5. Let the cake cool in the pan.
6. For the glaze, melt the sugar in a heavy saucepan until it sppears amber in colour.
7. Stir in the cream and salt and mix thoroughly. Keep over low heat until the desired smoothness is achieved.
8. Let the glaze cool down then sprinkle it over the cake just before you serve.

Nutritional Content of One Serving:
Calories: 400 Fat: 19.2g Protein: 4.9g Carbohydrates: 54.4g

Cardamom Carrot Cake

Total Time Taken: 1 ¼ hours
Yield: 16 Servings
Ingredients:

Cake:

- ¼ cup dark brown sugar
- ½ teaspoon baking powder
- ½ teaspoon salt
- 1 cup crushed pineapple
- 1 cup pecans, chopped
- 1 cup shredded coconut
- 1 cup vegetable oil
- 1 cup white sugar
- 1 teaspoon baking soda
- 1 teaspoon ground cardamom
- 1 teaspoon vanilla extract
- 2 cups all-purpose flour
- 2 cups grated carrots
- 4 eggs

Frosting:

- ½ cup butter, softened
- 1 cup cream cheese
- 1 cup powdered sugar
- 1 teaspoon vanilla extract

Directions:

1. For the cake, sift the flour, baking soda, baking powder, salt and cardamom in a container.
2. In a separate container, combine the eggs and sugars until creamy and fluffy.
3. Put in the vanilla, carrots, pineapple, coconut and pecans and mix thoroughly.
4. Fold in the dry ingredients then pour the batter into a 10- inch round cake pan coated with baking paper.
5. Preheat your oven and bake the cake for about fifty minutes or until it rises completely and is aromatic.
6. For the frosting, combine all the ingredients in a container for minimum five minutes.
7. Frost the chilled cake with the cream cheese buttercream and serve fresh or place in your refrigerator.

Nutritional Content of One Serving:

Calories: 416 Fat: 28.0g Protein: 4.6g Carbohydrates: 38.4g

Chai Spiced Cake

Total Time Taken: 1 ½ hours
Yield: 10 Servings
Ingredients:

Cake:

- ¼ teaspoon ground cloves
- ½ teaspoon ground ginger
- ½ teaspoon salt
- ½ teaspoon turmeric

- 1 ½ cups white sugar
- 1 cup butter, softened
- 1 teaspoon cinnamon powder
- 1 teaspoon vanilla extract
- 2 cups all-purpose flour
- 2 teaspoons baking powder
- 6 eggs

Frosting:
- ¼ cup light brown sugar
- ½ cup butter, softened
- 1 cup cream cheese
- 1 teaspoon grated ginger
- 2 cups powdered sugar

Directions:
1. For the cake, sift the flour with baking powder, salt and spices on a platter.
2. Mix the butter and sugar in a container until pale and thick.
3. Put in the eggs, one at a time, then mix in the dry ingredients, mixing gently using a spatula.
4. Spoon the batter in a 9-inch round cake pan coated with baking paper.
5. For the frosting, combine the cream cheese, butter and brown sugar in a container for minimum five minutes.
6. Put in the rest of the ingredients and mix thoroughly. Cover the cake with buttercream and serve fresh.

Nutritional Content of One Serving:
Calories: 484 Fat: 27.6g Protein: 5.7g Carbohydrates: 55.8g

Chai Spiced Streusel Cake

Total Time Taken: 1 hour
Yield: 10 Servings
Ingredients:

Streusel:
- ¼ cup all-purpose flour
- ¼ cup butter, melted
- ¼ cup light brown sugar
- ½ teaspoon cardamom powder
- ½ teaspoon cinnamon powder
- ½ teaspoon ground cloves
- ½ teaspoon star anise
- 1 cup pecans, chopped

Cake:
- ¼ cup butter, melted
- ¼ cup whole milk
- ½ cup white sugar

- 1 ¼ cups all-purpose flour
- 1 pinch salt
- 1 teaspoon baking powder
- 6 eggs, room temperature

Directions:

1. Mix the eggs, sugar and salt for minimum five minutes until its volume increases to almost three times it was.
2. Put in the milk then fold in the flour and baking powder.
3. Progressively mix in the melted butter then pour the batter in a 9-inch cake pan coated with baking paper.
4. For the streusel, combine all the ingredients in a container and stir thoroughly until grainy.
5. Spread the streusel over the cake and preheat your oven and bake at 350F for about forty minutes or until a golden-brown colour is achieved and fragrant.
6. Let cool in the pan and serve, sliced.

Nutritional Content of One Serving:

Calories: 254 Fat: 13.3g Protein: 5.7g Carbohydrates: 29.0g

Cherry Brownie Cake

Total Time Taken: 1 hour
Yield: 8 Servings
Ingredients:

- ¼ teaspoon salt
- ¾ cup butter
- ¾ cup light brown sugar
- 1 cup all-purpose flour
- 1 cup cherries, pitted
- 1 cup dark chocolate chips
- 1 teaspoon vanilla extract
- 3 eggs

Directions:

1. Mix the butter and chocolate chips in a heatproof container. Place over a hot water bath and melt them until the desired smoothness is achieved.
2. Turn off the heat and mix in the eggs, vanilla and sugar.
3. Fold in the flour and salt then pour the batter in a 8-inch round cake pan coated with baking paper.
4. Top with cherries and preheat your oven and bake at 350F for 20 minutes.
5. *The cake tastes best chilled.*

Nutritional Content of One Serving:

Calories: 367 Fat: 23.1g Protein: 4.9g Carbohydrates: 38.1g

Cherry Chocolate Cake

Total Time Taken: 1 ¼ hours
Yield: 10 Servings

Ingredients:

- ¼ teaspoon salt
- ½ cup butter, melted
- ½ cup milk
- ½ cup pine nuts, ground
- 1 ½ cups all-purpose flour
- 1 cup white sugar
- 1 teaspoon baking powder
- 1 teaspoon vanilla extract
- 2 cups cherries, pitted
- 3 eggs

Directions:

1. Mix the eggs and sugar in a container until volume increases to twice what it was.
2. Stir in the milk then progressively pour in the butter, stirring thoroughly.
3. Put in the vanilla then fold in the flour, baking powder and salt.
4. Put in the ground pine nuts then fold in the cherries.
5. Pour the batter in a 9-inch round cake pan coated with baking paper.
6. Pre-heat the oven and bake at 350F for about forty minutes or until a toothpick inserted into the center of the cake comes out clean.
7. Let the cake cool in the pan before you serve.

Nutritional Content of One Serving:

Calories: 314 Fat: 15.6g Protein: 5.1g Carbohydrates: 40.3g

Cherry Liqueur Soaked Cake

Total Time Taken: 1 ¼ hours
Yield: 8 Servings

Ingredients:

- ¼ cup cherry liqueurs
- ¼ cup dark brown sugar
- ¼ teaspoon salt
- ½ cup all-purpose flour
- ½ cup butter, melted
- ½ cup hot coffee
- ½ cup white sugar
- ½ teaspoon baking powder
- 1 ½ cups dark chocolate chips
- 1 cup almond flour
- 2 eggs

Directions:

1. Mix the coffee and chocolate in a container. Stir until melted and smooth.

2. Stir in the sugars, butter and eggs then fold in the almond flour, all-purpose flour, salt and baking powder.
3. Pour the batter in a 8-inch round cake pan coated with baking paper.
4. Pre-heat the oven and bake at 350F for a little more than half an hour.
5. Let the cake cool down then move to a platter.
6. Brush the cherry liqueur over the cake.
7. *The cake tastes best chilled.*

Nutritional Content of One Serving:
Calories: 343 Fat: 20.8g Protein: 4.6g Carbohydrates: 39.7g

Chestnut Puree Chocolate Cake

Total Time Taken: 1 ¼ hours
Yield: 10 Servings

Ingredients:

- ¼ cup butter
- ¼ teaspoon salt
- ½ cup canola oil
- ½ cup cocoa powder
- ½ cup ground almonds
- 1 cup all-purpose flour
- 1 cup chestnut puree
- 1 cup dark chocolate chips
- 1 cup white sugar
- 1 teaspoon baking powder

Directions:

1. Mix the canola oil, butter and chocolate chips in a heatproof container. Place over heatproof container and melt them together.
2. Turn off the heat and mix in the sugar and chestnut puree.
3. Fold in the cocoa powder, flour, almonds, salt and baking powder.
4. Spoon the batter in a 9-inch round cake pan coated with baking paper.
5. Pre-heat the oven and bake at 350F for around forty minutes or until a toothpick inserted into the center of the cake comes out clean.
6. The cake tastes best chilled.

Nutritional Content of One Serving:
Calories: 354 Fat: 21.8g Protein: 3.9g Carbohydrates: 41.6g

Chia Seed Chocolate Cake

Total Time Taken: 1 ¼ hours
Yield: 10 Servings

Ingredients:

- ¼ cup cocoa powder
- ¼ teaspoon salt

18

- ½ cup butter
- ½ cup dark chocolate chips
- 1 ½ cups all-purpose flour
- 1 cup canola oil
- 1 cup white sugar
- 1 tablespoon orange zest
- 1 teaspoon baking powder
- 2 tablespoons chia seeds
- 3 eggs

Directions:

1. Melt the chocolate and butter in a container until the desired smoothness is achieved.
2. Turn off the heat and mix in the eggs, orange zest, sugar and canola oil.
3. Fold in the cocoa powder, chia seeds, flour, baking powder and salt then pour the batter in a 9-inch round cake pan coated with baking paper.
4. Pre-heat the oven and bake at 350F for around forty minutes or until a toothpick inserted into the center of the cake comes out clean.
5. *The cake tastes best chilled.*

Nutritional Content of One Serving:

Calories: 470 Fat: 34.4g Protein: 4.5g Carbohydrates: 40.0g

Chocolate Biscuit Cake

Total Time Taken: 3 hours
Yield: 10 Servings
Ingredients:

- ¼ cup cocoa powder
- ¼ cup dried cranberries
- ½ cup butter
- ½ cup dark chocolate chips
- ½ cup golden syrup
- ½ cup milk chocolate chips
- ½ cup pecans, chopped
- 1 cup golden raisins
- 1 cup heavy cream
- 1 cup milk
- 10 oz. digestive biscuits, chopped

Directions:

1. Melt the chocolate chips and butter in a heatproof container over a hot water bath.
2. Mix the cream, milk and cocoa powder and place over low heat. Bring to a boil and cook just until slightly thickened. Turn off the heat and mix in the chocolate mixture.
3. Mix this mixture with the remaining ingredients in a container then transfer in a 8-inch cake pan coated with plastic wrap.

4. Place in your refrigerator to set for about two hours then serve, sliced.

Nutritional Content of One Serving:

Calories: 408 Fat: 24.0g Protein: 4.3g Carbohydrates: 49.1g

Chocolate Bundt Cake

Total Time Taken: 1 ¼ hours
Yield: 10 Servings

Ingredients:

- ½ cup butter, softened
- ½ cup cocoa powder
- ½ cup dark chocolate chips
- ½ teaspoon baking soda
- ½ teaspoon salt
- 1 ½ cups all-purpose flour
- 1 cup white sugar
- 1 teaspoon baking powder
- 1 teaspoon vanilla extract
- 2 tablespoons canola oil
- 3 eggs

Directions:

1. Mix the butter, canola oil and sugar in a container until light and pale.
2. Stir in the eggs and vanilla and mix thoroughly.
3. Fold in the flour, cocoa powder, baking powder, baking soda and salt.
4. Put in the chocolate chips then spoon the batter in a greased Bundt cake pan.
5. Pre-heat the oven and bake at 350F for about forty minutes or until well risen and it passes the toothpick test.
6. Let the cake cool in the pan and serve, sliced.

Nutritional Content of One Serving:

Calories: 308 Fat: 15.7g Protein: 4.9g Carbohydrates: 41.1g

Chocolate Chip Blackberry Cake

Total Time Taken: 1 ¼ hours
Yield: 10 Servings

Ingredients:

- ¼ cup canola oil
- ¼ cup cornstarch
- ¼ teaspoon salt
- ½ cup butter, softened
- ½ cup dark chocolate chips
- ½ cup plain yogurt
- 1 ½ cups all-purpose flour

- 1 cup fresh blackberries
- 1 cup white sugar
- 1 teaspoon baking powder
- 3 eggs

Directions:

1. Mix the butter, oil and sugar in a container until creamy and fluffy.
2. Put in the eggs and yogurt and mix thoroughly.
3. Fold in the flour, cornstarch, baking powder and salt and mix using a spatula.
4. Put in the chocolate chips and blackberries then spoon the batter in a 9-inch round cake pan coated with baking paper.
5. Preheat your oven and bake the cake for about forty minutes or until it rises significantly and starts to appear golden-brown.
6. Let the cake cool in the pan before you serve.

Nutritional Content of One Serving:

Calories: 347 Fat: 18.0 Protein: 5.0g Carbohydrates: 43.8g

Chocolate Chip Bundt Cake

Total Time Taken: 1 ¼ hours
Yield: 12 Servings

Ingredients:

- ½ teaspoon salt
- ¾ cup dark chocolate chips
- 1 cup butter, softened
- 1 cup plain yogurt
- 1 cup white sugar
- 1 teaspoon vanilla extract
- 2 cups all-purpose flour
- 2 teaspoons baking powder
- 3 eggs

Directions:

1. Mix the flour with baking powder and salt.
2. Mix the butter with sugar until creamy. Put in the eggs, one at a time, then mix in the vanilla and mix thoroughly.
3. Put in the yogurt and mix thoroughly then fold in the flour, followed by the chocolate chips.
4. Spoon the batter in a greased Bundt cake pan.
5. Pre-heat the oven and bake at 350F for about forty minutes or until a toothpick inserted in the cake comes out clean.

Nutritional Content of One Serving:

Calories: 341 Fat: 18.9g Protein: 5.3g Carbohydrates: 39.5g

Chocolate Chip Pumpkin Bundt Cake

Total Time Taken: 1 ¼ hours
Yield: 12 Servings

Ingredients:

- ½ teaspoon salt
- 1 ½ cups white sugar
- 1 ½ teaspoons baking powder
- 1 cup butter, softened
- 1 cup dark chocolate chips
- 1 cup pumpkin puree
- 1 teaspoon vanilla extract
- 2 cups all-purpose flour
- 2 eggs
- 2 tablespoons molasses

Directions:

1. Mix the butter, sugar and molasses in a container until creamy and light.
2. Stir in the vanilla and eggs, as well as the pumpkin puree.
3. Fold in the remaining ingredients and stir lightly.
4. Spoon the batter in a greased Bundt cake pan. Pre-heat the oven and bake at 350F for about forty-five minutes or until a toothpick inserted into the center of the cake comes out clean.
5. Let the cake cool in the pan before you serve.

Nutritional Content of One Serving:

Calories: 381 Fat: 19.0g Protein: 4.1g Carbohydrates: 52.1g

Chocolate Coconut Cake

Total Time Taken: 1 ¼ hours
Yield: 10 Servings

Ingredients:

- ¼ cup cocoa powder
- ¼ teaspoon salt
- ½ cup butter
- ¾ cup milk
- 1 ½ cups all-purpose flour
- 1 cup shredded coconut
- 1 cup white sugar
- 1 teaspoon baking powder
- 2 eggs
- 2 tablespoons canola oil

Directions:

1. Mix the butter, oil and sugar in a container until fluffy and creamy.

2. Put in the eggs, one at a time, then mix in the milk.
3. Put in the dry ingredients and stir lightly using a spatula.
4. Spoon the batter in a 8-inch round cake pan coated with baking paper.
5. Pre-heat the oven and bake at 350F for around forty minutes or until a toothpick inserted into the center of the cake comes out clean.
6. *The cake tastes best chilled.*

Nutritional Content of One Serving:
Calories: 305 Fat: 16.4g Protein: 4.4g Carbohydrates: 37.9g

Chocolate Coffee Cake

Total Time Taken: 1 hour
Yield: 12 Servings
Ingredients:

Cake:
- ½ cup canola oil
- ½ teaspoon salt
- 1 cup buttermilk
- 1 cup hot coffee
- 1 cup white sugar
- 2 cups all-purpose flour
- 2 teaspoons baking powder
- 2 teaspoons instant coffee
- 3 eggs

Frosting:
- 1 cup heavy cream
- 2 cups dark chocolate chips
- 2 teaspoons instant coffee

Directions:
1. For the cake, combine the buttermilk, canola oil, hot coffee and eggs in a container.
2. Stir in the dry ingredients and mix thoroughly.
3. Pour the batter in a 9-inch round cake pan coated with baking paper.
4. Pre-heat the oven and bake at 350F for about fifty minutes.
5. When finished, transfer the chilled cake on a platter.
6. For the frosting, bring the cream to the boiling point in a saucepan. Put in the chocolate and stir until it melts completely. Stir in the coffee.
7. Cover the cake with chocolate coffee frosting and serve it fresh.

Nutritional Content of One Serving:
Calories: 371 Fat: 19.6g Protein: 5.8g Carbohydrates: 47.6g

Chocolate Dulce De Leche Cake

Total Time Taken: 1 ¼ hours
Yield: 12 Servings

23

Ingredients:

- ½ cup butter, softened
- ½ cup canola oil
- ½ cup dulce de leche
- ½ cup sour cream
- ½ teaspoon salt
- 1 ¾ cups all-purpose flour
- 1 cup dark chocolate chips
- 1 cup white sugar
- 2 teaspoons baking powder
- 3 eggs

Directions:

1. Mix the butter and oil in a container. Put in the sugar and stir thoroughly until creamy.
2. Put in the eggs and sour cream and mix thoroughly.
3. Fold in the flour, baking powder and salt then put in the chocolate chips. Pour the batter in a 9-inch round cake pan coated with baking paper.
4. Drop spoonfuls of dulce de leche over the batter and preheat your oven and bake at 350F for about forty minutes or until a toothpick inserted into the center of the cake comes out clean.
5. *The cake tastes best chilled.*

Nutritional Content of One Serving:

Calories: 397 Fat: 23.2g Protein: 5.0g Carbohydrates: 45.8g

Chocolate Fudge Cake

Total Time Taken: 1 ½ hours
Yield: 12 Servings
Ingredients:

Cake:

- ¼ cup cocoa powder
- ¼ teaspoon salt
- ½ cup dark chocolate chips
- 1 cup hot water
- ½ cup sour cream
- ½ teaspoon baking soda
- ¾ cup butter, softened
- 1 ½ teaspoons baking powder
- 1 ¾ cups all-purpose flour
- 1 cup dark brown sugar
- 2 eggs
- 2 tablespoons vegetable oil
- 1 teaspoon vanilla extract

Frosting:

- ½ cup cocoa powder
- 1 pinch salt
- 1 cup butter, softened
- 2 cups powdered sugar
- 2 tablespoons whole milk

Directions:

1. To prepare the cake, combine the chocolate chips, hot water and cocoa powder in a container.
2. In a separate container, combine the butter and sugar until creamy and pale. Stir in the eggs, one at a time, then put in the sour cream, vanilla and oil.
3. Mix the flour with baking powder, baking soda and salt then mix it with the butter mixture alternating it with the chocolate mixture. Begin and finish with flour.
4. Split the batter between two 9-inch circular cake pans covered with parchment paper.
5. Pre-heat the oven and bake at 350F for about half an hour.
6. Let cool and then take the cakes out of the pans and let them sit on the side you perform the next few steps.
7. For the frosting: combine the butter and powdered sugar for minimum five minutes until creamy and fluffy.
8. Put in the cocoa powder, salt and milk and stir thoroughly for another five minutes.
9. Use half of the frosting to fill the cake then garnish it with the half that is left over.
    10. Serve immediately or place in your fridge until it is time to serve.

Nutritional Content of One Serving:

Calories: 517 Fat: 34.2g Protein: 4.8g Carbohydrates: 52.9g

Chocolate Hazelnut Cake

Total Time Taken: 1 ¼ hours
Yield: 10 Servings
Ingredients:

Cake:

- ½ cup cocoa powder
- ½ teaspoon baking powder
- ½ teaspoon salt
- 1 cup all-purpose flour
- 1 cup ground hazelnuts
- 1 cup white sugar
- 6 eggs

Glaze:

- ½ cup heavy cream
- 1 cup dark chocolate chips

Directions:

1. To prepare the cake, combine the eggs with sugar until fluffy, minimum volume increases to twice what it was.

2. Fold in the flour, cocoa powder, baking powder, salt and hazelnuts then pour the batter in a 9-inch round cake pan coated with baking paper.
3. Preheat your oven and bake the cake for forty minutes or until a toothpick inserted in the center comes out clean.
4. Let the cake cool in the pan then move to a platter.
5. For the glaze, bring the cream to the boiling point then put in the chocolate and mix thoroughly.
6. Pour the warm glaze over the cake. Serve immediately or place in your refrigerator.

Nutritional Content of One Serving:
Calories: 292 Fat: 13.3g Protein: 7.4g Carbohydrates: 41.6g

Chocolate Hazelnut Cake

Total Time Taken: 1 ¼ hours
Yield: 10 Servings
Ingredients:
- ¼ cup heavy cream
- ½ cup cherry jam
- ½ cup cocoa powder
- ½ cup white sugar
- ½ teaspoon baking soda
- ½ teaspoon salt
- 1 cup all-purpose flour
- 1 cup ground hazelnuts
- 1 teaspoon baking powder
- 2 whole eggs
- 6 egg yolks

Directions:
1. Mix the hazelnuts, flour, baking powder, baking soda and salt in a container. Put in the cocoa powder as well.
2. Mix the eggs, egg yolks and sugar in a container until thickened and fluffy. Stir in the cream and cherry jam.
3. Fold in the flour then spoon the cake in a 8-inch round cake pan coated with baking paper.
4. Pre-heat the oven and bake at 350F for around forty minutes or until a toothpick inserted into the center of the cake comes out clean.
5. The cake tastes best chilled.

Nutritional Content of One Serving:
Calories: 240 Fat: 9.9g Protein: 6.0g Carbohydrates: 34.9g

Chocolate Mousse Cake

Total Time Taken: 1 ½ hours
Yield: 10 Servings
Ingredients:
Cake:

- ¼ cup cocoa powder
- ¼ cup heavy cream
- ¼ teaspoon salt
- ½ cup dark chocolate chips
- 1 cup all-purpose flour
- 1 cup buttermilk
- 1 egg
- 1 teaspoon baking powder

Chocolate mousse:
- ½ cup heavy cream, heated
- 1 cup dark chocolate chips
- 1 cup heavy cream, whipped

Directions:
1. For the cake, melt the cream and chocolate together in a heatproof container.
2. Stir in the remaining ingredients and stir for a few seconds to mix.
3. Pour the batter in a 9-inch round cake pan coated with baking paper.
4. Pre-heat the oven and bake at 350F for around forty minutes or until well risen and fragrant.
5. When finished, move the cake to a cake ring and place it on a platter.
6. For the chocolate mousse, combine the cream and chocolate chips in a container. Stir until melted and smooth. Let cool down.
7. Fold in the whipped cream then pour the mousse over the cake.
8. *Chill the cake before you serve.*

Nutritional Content of One Serving:
Calories: 223 Fat: 13.6g Protein: 4.7g Carbohydrates: 24.7g

Chocolate Nutella Cake

Total Time Taken: 1 ½ hours
Yield: 10 Servings
Ingredients:
- ½ cup brewed coffee
- ½ cup canola oil
- ½ teaspoon salt
- 1 cup ground hazelnuts
- 1 cup Nutella
- 1 cup whole milk
- 1 teaspoon vanilla extract
- 2 cups all-purpose flour
- 2 eggs
- 2 tablespoons Kahlua
- 2 teaspoons baking powder

Directions:

1. Mix the ground hazelnuts, flour, baking powder and salt in a container.
2. Mix the eggs, milk, canola oil, Kahlua, vanilla and coffee in a separate container. Stir in the flour mixture then spoon the batter in a 9-inch round cake pan coated with baking paper.
3. Drop spoonfuls of Nutella over the batter and preheat your oven and bake at 350F for about forty minutes or until a toothpick inserted into the center of the cake comes out clean.
4. *The cake tastes best chilled.*

Nutritional Content of One Serving:

Calories: 295 Fat: 18.5g Protein: 5.8g Carbohydrates: 25.4g

Chocolate Olive Oil Cake

Total Time Taken: 1 ¼ hours
Yield: 10 Servings

Ingredients:

- ¼ cup whole milk
- ¼ teaspoon salt
- ½ cup cocoa powder
- 1 cup all-purpose flour
- 1 cup white sugar
- 1 teaspoon baking powder
- 1 teaspoon orange zest
- 1 teaspoon vanilla extract
- 2 eggs
- 2/3 cup olive oil

Directions:

1. Mix the eggs with sugar until fluffy and pale. Stir in the vanilla and orange zest and mix thoroughly.
2. Put in the olive oil and milk then fold in the cocoa powder, flour, salt and baking powder.
3. Pour the batter in a 8-inch round cake pan coated with baking paper.
4. Pre-heat the oven and bake at 350F for forty minutes or until a toothpick inserted in the center comes out clean.
5. *The cake tastes best chilled.*

Nutritional Content of One Serving:

Calories: 263 Fat: 15.2g Protein: 3.4g Carbohydrates: 32.6g

Chocolate Peanut Butter Bundt Cake

Total Time Taken: 1 ¼ hours
Yield: 10 Servings

Ingredients:

- ¼ cup whole milk
- ½ cup cocoa powder
- ½ teaspoon salt

- 1 ½ cups all-purpose flour
- 1 cup butter, softened
- 1 cup light brown sugar
- 1 cup sour cream
- 1 teaspoon baking powder
- 1 teaspoon baking soda
- 1 teaspoon vanilla extract
- 2/3 cup smooth peanut butter
- 3 eggs

Directions:

1. Mix the butter, sugar and vanilla in a container until fluffy and creamy.
2. Put in the eggs, one at a time, then mix in the sour cream and milk.
3. Fold in the flour, cocoa powder, baking powder, baking soda and salt.
4. Spoon half of the batter in a greased Bundt cake pan. Top with spoonfuls of peanut butter then cover with the rest of the batter.
5. Pre-heat the oven and bake at 350F for about forty minutes or until a toothpick inserted into the center of the cake comes out clean.
6. *The cake tastes best chilled.*

Nutritional Content of One Serving:

Calories: 470 Fat: 34.1g Protein: 9.8g Carbohydrates: 35.9g

Chocolate Peppermint Cake

Total Time Taken: 1 ½ hours
Yield: 8 Servings
Ingredients:

Cake:

- ¼ teaspoon salt
- ½ cup butter, cubed
- ½ cup light brown sugar
- 1 cup all-purpose flour
- 1 cup dark chocolate chips
- 1 teaspoon baking powder
- 2 eggs
- 2 tablespoons cocoa powder

Glaze:

- ¼ cup heavy cream
- ¼ cup whole milk
- 1 pinch salt
- 3 tablespoons cocoa powder

Directions:

1. For the cake, combine the chocolate chips and butter in a heatproof container and place over a hot water bath. Melt them together until the desired smoothness is achieved.
2. Put in the sugar and eggs and mix thoroughly.
3. Stir in the flour, cocoa powder, baking powder and salt. Pour the batter in a 8-inch round cake pan coated with baking paper.
4. Pre-heat the oven and bake at 350F for about half an hour.
5. For the glaze, combine all the ingredients in a saucepan and place over low heat. Cook until it becomes thick.
6. Sprinkle the glaze over the cake and serve chilled.

Nutritional Content of One Serving:

Calories: 304 Fat: 18.8g Protein: 5.1g Carbohydrates: 33.5g

Chocolate Pumpkin Cake

Total Time Taken: 1 hour
Yield: 10 Servings
Ingredients:

- ½ cup buttermilk
- ½ cup cocoa powder
- ½ cup sour cream
- ½ teaspoon ground star anise
- ½ teaspoon salt
- 1 cup butter, softened
- 1 cup light brown sugar
- 1 cup pumpkin puree
- 1 teaspoon baking powder
- 1 teaspoon baking soda
- 1 teaspoon ground cinnamon
- 1 teaspoon ground ginger
- 1 teaspoon vanilla extract
- 2 cups all-purpose flour
- 4 eggs

Directions:

1. Mix the butter and sugar in a container until fluffy and creamy.
2. Stir in the eggs, one at a time, then put in the vanilla, pumpkin puree, sour cream and buttermilk and mix thoroughly.
3. Fold in the dry ingredients then spoon the batter in a 10-inch round cake pan coated with baking paper.
4. Preheat your oven and bake the cake for about fifty minutes or until a toothpick inserted in the center comes out clean.
5. Let the cake cool in the pan and serve, sliced.

Nutritional Content of One Serving:

Calories: 385 Fat: 23.6g Protein: 6.9g Carbohydrates: 39.6g

Cakey Blueberry Muffins

Total Time Taken: 1 hour
Yield: 12 Servings
Ingredients:

- ¼ cup cornstarch
- ¼ teaspoon salt
- ½ cup canola oil
- ¾ cup white sugar
- 1 ½ cups all-purpose flour
- 1 ½ teaspoons baking powder
- 1 cup blueberries
- 1 teaspoon vanilla extract
- 2 eggs
- 2/3 cup sour cream

Directions:

1. Mix the eggs and sugar in a container until volume increases to twice what it was. Stir in the vanilla and oil and mix thoroughly then put in the sour cream and stir thoroughly until blended.
2. Fold in the flour, cornstarch, salt and baking powder then fold in the blueberries.
3. Spoon the batter in a muffin tin covered with muffin papers.
4. Pre-heat the oven and bake at 350F for about twenty minutes or until a toothpick inserted into them comes out dry.

These muffins taste best chilled.

Nutritional Content of One Serving:
Calories: 241 Fat: 12.7g Protein: 3.0g Carbohydrates: 29.6g

Caramel Vanilla Cupcakes

Total Time Taken: 1 ½ hours
Yield: 12 Servings
Ingredients:

Cupcakes:

- 2 eggs
- 1/3 cup butter, melted
- 1 teaspoon vanilla extract
- 1 egg
- 1 cup milk
- 1 ¾ cups all-purpose flour
- 1 ½ teaspoons baking powder
- ¼ teaspoon salt

Frosting:

- 2 cups powdered sugar

- 1 teaspoon vanilla extract
- 1 cup butter, softened
- ½ cup caramel sauce

Directions:

1. To make the cupcakes, combine the flour, salt and baking powder in a container.
2. Combine the eggs, butter, milk, egg and vanilla then pour this mixture over the flour. Give it a quick mix then spoon the batter in a muffin tin covered with muffin papers.
3. Pre-heat the oven and bake at 350F for about twenty minutes or until it rises significantly and starts to appear golden-brown. Let them cool down.
4. To make the frosting, combine the butter in a container until fluffy. Put in the sugar and vanilla and keep mixing for five minutes.
5. Pipe the frosting over the cupcakes and sprinkle them with caramel sauce.

These cupcakes taste best when fresh.

Nutritional Content of One Serving:

Calories: 388 Fat: 22.2g Protein: 4.3g Carbohydrates: 44.3g

Caribbean Muffins

Total Time Taken: 1 hour
Yield: 12 Servings
Ingredients:

- ¼ cup wheat bran
- ¼ teaspoon salt
- ½ cup shredded coconut
- 1 ½ cups all-purpose flour
- 1 ½ teaspoons baking powder
- 1 cup buttermilk
- 1 cup crushed pineapple
- 1 egg
- 1 mango, peeled and diced
- 2 tablespoons chia seeds

Directions:

1. Mix the flour, wheat bran, salt, baking powder, chia seeds and coconut in a container.
2. Put in the egg, buttermilk and pineapple and mix thoroughly.
3. Fold in the mango then spoon the batter in a muffin tin covered with muffin papers.
4. Preheat your oven and bake the muffins at 350F for about twenty minutes or until it rises significantly and starts to appear golden-brown.

These muffins taste best chilled.

Nutritional Content of One Serving:

Calories: 130 Fat: 3.5g Protein: 4.3g Carbohydrates: 21.0g

Carrot Cake Pecan Muffins

Total Time Taken: 1 hour
Yield: 12 Servings
Ingredients:

- ¼ teaspoon salt
- ½ cup canola oil
- ½ cup crushed pineapple
- ½ cup light brown sugar
- ½ cup milk
- ½ cup walnuts, chopped
- ½ teaspoon ground ginger
- 1 ½ cups all-purpose flour
- 1 cup grated carrot
- 1 egg
- 1 teaspoon baking soda
- 1 teaspoon cinnamon powder

Directions:

1. Mix the flour, salt, baking soda, cinnamon and ginger.
2. Put in the milk, egg, oil, sugar, carrot, pineapple and walnuts and mix thoroughly.
3. Spoon the batter in a muffin tin covered with muffin papers.
4. Pre-heat the oven and bake at 350F for about twenty minutes or until it rises significantly and becomes aromatic.
5. Serve the muffins chilled or store them in an airtight container for maximum four days.

Nutritional Content of One Serving:
Calories: 210 Fat: 12.9g Protein: 3.8g Carbohydrates: 20.8g

Carrot White Chocolate Muffins

Total Time Taken: 1 hour
Yield: 12 Servings
Ingredients:

- ¼ cup canola oil
- ¼ teaspoon baking soda
- ½ cup plain yogurt
- ½ cup white chocolate chips
- ½ cup white sugar
- ½ cup whole wheat flour
- ½ teaspoon salt
- ½ teaspoon salt
- 1 cup all-purpose flour
- 1 cup crushed pineapple

- 1 cup grated carrots
- 1 egg
- 1 teaspoon baking powder

Directions:

1. Mix the egg and sugar in a container until pale and light.
2. Put in the oil and yogurt and mix thoroughly.
3. Fold in the flours, salt, baking powder, baking soda and salt.
4. Put in the crushed pineapple, carrots and chocolate chips.
5. Spoon the batter in a muffin tin covered with muffin papers and preheat your oven and bake at 350F for about twenty minutes or until a toothpick inserted into the center of a muffin comes out clean.

These muffins taste best chilled.

Nutritional Content of One Serving:

Calories: 190 Fat: 7.5g Protein: 3.2g Carbohydrates: 28.1g

Chai Vanilla Frosted Cupcakes

Total Time Taken: 1 ½ hours
Yield: 12 Servings
Ingredients:

Cupcakes:

- ½ cup butter, softened
- 2 eggs
- 1 teaspoon vanilla extract
- 1 ½ cups all-purpose flour
- 1 teaspoon baking powder
- ½ teaspoon baking soda
- ¼ teaspoon cinnamon powder
- ¼ teaspoon ground ginger
- ¼ teaspoon ground star anise
- ¼ teaspoon ground cardamom
- 2/3 cup white sugar
- 2/3 cup buttermilk

Frosting:

- 1 cup butter, softened
- 1 teaspoon vanilla extract
- 2 cups powdered sugar

Directions:

1. To make the cupcakes, combine the butter and sugar in a container until creamy and firm.
2. Put in the eggs and vanilla, then mix in the buttermilk.
3. Put in the flour, baking powder, baking soda, cinnamon powder, ginger, star anise and cardamom, as well as a pinch of salt.

4. Pour the batter in a muffin tin covered with muffin papers and preheat your oven and bake at 350F for about twenty minutes or until a golden-brown colour is achieved.
5. Let cool down in the pan.
6. To make the frosting, combine the butter in a container until creamy and light.
7. Put in the sugar, ½ cup at a time, and stir thoroughly for at least five minutes.
8. Put in the vanilla and mix thoroughly.
9. Top each cupcake with the frosting and serve fresh.

Nutritional Content of One Serving:
Calories: 399 Fat: 24.0g Protein: 3.2g Carbohydrates: 44.1g

Cherry Coconut Muffins

Total Time Taken: 1 hour
Yield: 12 Servings
Ingredients:

- ¼ cup canola oil
- ½ cup white sugar
- ½ teaspoon salt
- ¾ cup coconut milk
- 1 cup all-purpose flour
- 1 cup cherries, pitted
- 1 cup shredded coconut
- 1 teaspoon baking soda
- 2 eggs

Directions:

1. Mix the eggs and sugar in a container until fluffy and pale. Put in the oil and milk and mix thoroughly.
2. Fold in the coconut, flour, salt, baking soda and cherries.
3. Spoon the batter in a muffin tin covered with muffin papers.
4. Preheat your oven and bake the muffins at 350F for about twenty minutes or until a toothpick inserted into them comes out dry.

These muffins taste best chilled.

Nutritional Content of One Serving:
Calories: 185 Fat: 11.2g Protein: 2.6g Carbohydrates: 19.9g

Cherry Muffins

Total Time Taken: 1 hour
Yield: 10 Servings
Ingredients:

- ¼ teaspoon salt
- ½ cup butter, melted
- ½ cup white sugar
- 1 cup all-purpose flour
- 1 cup cherries, pitted

- 1 teaspoon baking powder
- 1 teaspoon vanilla extract
- 4 eggs

Directions:

1. Mix the eggs, sugar and vanilla in a container until its volume increases to almost three times it was.
2. Stir in the butter and mix thoroughly.
3. Fold in the flour, salt and baking powder.
4. Put in the cherries then spoon the batter in a muffin tin covered with muffin papers.
5. Preheat your oven and bake the muffins at 350F for about twenty minutes or until a golden-brown colour is achieved and it rises significantly.

These muffins taste best chilled.

Nutritional Content of One Serving:

Calories: 200 Fat: 11.1g Protein: 3.6g Carbohydrates: 22.0g

Chocolate Avocado Cupcakes

Total Time Taken: 1 ½ hours
Yield: 12 Servings
Ingredients:

Cupcakes:

- 1 large avocado, mashed
- 1 cup coconut milk
- 1 teaspoon vanilla extract
- 1 egg
- 2 egg whites
- 1 cup whole wheat flour
- 1 cup all-purpose flour
- ¼ teaspoon salt
- 2 teaspoons baking powder
- ½ cup cocoa powder
- 2/3 cup coconut sugar

Frosting:

- ¼ cup cocoa powder
- ½ teaspoon vanilla extract
- 1 large avocado, mashed
- 2 tablespoons coconut oil
- 2 tablespoons coconut sugar

Directions:

1. To make the cupcakes, combine the avocado, coconut sugar, coconut milk, vanilla, egg and egg whites in a container until creamy.
2. Put in the remaining ingredients and stir swiftly to combine.
3. Spoon the batter in a muffin tin covered with muffin papers.

4. Pre-heat the oven and bake at 350F for about twenty minutes or until a toothpick inserted in the muffins comes out clean.
5. Let cool in the pan.
6. To make the frosting, combine all the ingredients in a blender or food processor and pulse until well mixed.
7. Pipe the frosting over each cupcake and serve fresh.

Nutritional Content of One Serving:

Calories: 280 Fat: 14.8g Protein: 5.3g Carbohydrates: 36.0g

Chocolate Candied Orange Muffins

Total Time Taken: 1 hour
Yield: 12 Servings
Ingredients:

- ¼ cup candied orange peel, chopped
- ½ cup canola oil
- ½ cup dark chocolate chips
- ½ cup fresh orange juice
- ½ cup plain yogurt
- ½ cup white sugar
- ½ teaspoon salt
- 1 ½ cups all-purpose flour
- 1 ½ teaspoons baking powder
- 1 teaspoon orange zest
- 2 eggs

Directions:

1. Mix the sugar, orange juice, eggs, oil, yogurt and orange zest in a container.
2. Stir in the flour, salt, baking powder, chocolate chips and orange peel and mix using a spatula.
3. Pour the batter in a muffin tin covered with muffin papers and preheat your oven and bake at 350F for about twenty minutes or until a toothpick inserted into them comes out dry.

These muffins taste best chilled.

Nutritional Content of One Serving:

Calories: 217

Fat:11.4g Protein: 3.5g Carbohydrates: 26.3g

Chocolate Chip Cinnamon Muffins

Total Time Taken: 1 hour
Yield: 12 Servings
Ingredients:

- ¼ cup milk
- ½ cup butter, melted
- ½ cup dark chocolate chips
- ½ cup white sugar

- ½ teaspoon salt
- 1 cup all-purpose flour
- 1 teaspoon baking powder
- 1 teaspoon cinnamon powder
- 1 teaspoon orange zest
- 1 teaspoon vanilla extract
- 2 tablespoons dark brown sugar
- 4 eggs

Directions:

1. Mix the eggs and sugars in a container until fluffy and pale.
2. Put in the vanilla, orange zest and melted butter.
3. Fold in the flour, cinnamon, salt and baking powder then put in the milk and chocolate chips.
4. Spoon the batter in a muffin tin covered with muffin papers.
5. Pre-heat the oven and bake at 350F for about twenty minutes or until a golden-brown colour is achieved and it rises significantly.

These muffins taste best chilled.

Nutritional Content of One Serving:

Calories: 191 Fat: 10.7g Protein: 3.5g Carbohydrates: 21.7g

Chocolate Chip Muffins

Total Time Taken: 1 hour
Yield: 12 Servings
Ingredients:

- ½ cup canola oil
- ½ cup chocolate chips
- ½ cup white sugar
- ½ teaspoon salt
- 1 ½ teaspoons baking powder
- 1 cup all-purpose flour
- 1 cup whole wheat flour
- 1 egg
- 1 teaspoon vanilla extract
- 2/3 cup milk

Directions:

1. Mix the flours, baking powder and salt in a container.
2. Put in the sugar, egg, milk, oil and vanilla and mix using a spatula.
3. Fold in the chocolate chips then spoon the batter in a muffin tin covered with muffin papers.
4. Preheat your oven and bake the muffins at 350F for about twenty minutes or until a golden-brown colour is achieved and it rises significantly.

These muffins taste best chilled.

Nutritional Content of One Serving:

Calories: 238 Fat: 12.0g Protein: 3.6g Carbohydrates: 29.4g

Chocolate Chunk Cupcakes

Total Time Taken: 1 ½ hours
Yield: 12 Servings
Ingredients:

Cupcakes:

- ½ cup butter, melted
- ½ cup sour cream
- ½ cup white sugar
- ½ teaspoon salt
- 2 cups all-purpose flour
- 2 eggs
- 2 teaspoons baking powder
- 4 oz. dark chocolate, chopped

Frosting:

- 1 ½ cups heavy cream, whipped
- 2 oz. dark chocolate, chopped

Directions:

1. To make the cupcakes, combine the butter, sugar and eggs in a container until pale.
2. Put in the sour cream and mix thoroughly.
3. Fold in the flour, baking powder and salt then fold in the dark chocolate.
4. Spoon the batter in a muffin tin covered with muffin papers.
5. Preheat your oven and bake the cupcakes at 350F for about twenty minutes or until a golden-brown colour is achieved and it rises significantly.
6. Let the cupcakes cool then top each of them with a dollop of whipped cream.
7. Drizzle each cream with chopped chocolate and serve.

Nutritional Content of One Serving:
Calories: 334 Fat: 20.4g Protein: 4.8g Carbohydrates: 33.9g

Chocolate Cupcakes With Peanut Butter Frosting

Total Time Taken: 1 ½ hours
Yield: 16 Servings
Ingredients:

Cupcakes:

- ¼ teaspoon salt
- ½ cup butter, softened
- ½ cup cocoa powder
- ½ cup sour cream
- 1 ½ cups all-purpose flour

- 1 ½ teaspoons baking powder
- 1 cup buttermilk
- 1 cup white sugar
- 1 teaspoon vanilla extract
- 3 eggs

Frosting:
- ½ cup butter, softened
- 1 cup powdered sugar
- 1 cup smooth peanut butter
- 1 teaspoon vanilla extract
- 2 tablespoons heavy cream

Directions:
1. To make the cupcakes, combine the butter and sugar in a container until creamy and pale.
2. Put in the eggs and mix thoroughly then mix in the vanilla, sour cream and buttermilk.
3. Fold in the flour, cocoa powder, salt and baking powder then spoon the batter in a muffin tin covered with muffin papers.
4. Preheat your oven and bake the muffins at 350F for about twenty minutes.
5. Let the cupcakes cool down.
6. To make the frosting, combine the peanut butter, butter and sugar in a container until fluffy and pale.
7. Put in the vanilla and cream and continue whipping for five minutes until fluffy and airy.
8. Garnish the cupcakes with the peanut butter frosting.

These cupcakes taste best when fresh.

Nutritional Content of One Serving:
Calories: 363 Fat: 23.3g Protein: 7.7g Carbohydrates: 35.0g

Chocolate Drizzle **Cupcakes**

Total Time Taken: 1 ½ hours
Yield: 12 Servings
Ingredients:
Cupcakes:
- ¼ cup brewed coffee
- ¼ cup canola oil
- ¼ cup cocoa powder
- ½ teaspoon salt
- 1 ½ cups all-purpose flour
- 1 ½ teaspoons baking powder
- 1 cup buttermilk
- 1 teaspoon vanilla extract
- 2 eggs

Frosting:
- 1 cup butter, softened

- 1 tablespoon cocoa powder
- 1 tablespoon dark rum
- 2 cups powdered sugar

Directions:

1. To make the cupcakes, combine the flour, salt, baking powder and cocoa powder in a container.
2. Put in the eggs, vanilla, buttermilk, coffee and canola oil and stir for a few seconds to mix.
3. Pour the batter in 12 muffin cups covered with muffin papers and preheat your oven and bake at 350F for about twenty minutes or until a toothpick inserted into them comes out dry.
4. Let cool down.
5. To make the frosting, combine the butter until fluffy. Put in the sugar and mix for about five to seven minutes or until pale and light.
6. Stir in the rum and mix thoroughly.
7. Top each cupcake with the frosting and serve them fresh.

Nutritional Content of One Serving:

Calories: 338 Fat: 21.3g Protein: 3.8g Carbohydrates: 34.5g

Chocolate Graham Cupcakes

Total Time Taken: 1 ½ hours
Yield: 12 Servings
Ingredients:

Cupcakes:

- ¼ cup whole milk
- ½ cup all-purpose flour
- ½ cup crushed graham crackers
- ½ teaspoon salt
- 1 cup butter, softened
- 1 cup light brown sugar
- 1 cup whole wheat flour
- 1 teaspoon baking soda
- 1 teaspoon vanilla extract
- 1/2 teaspoon cinnamon powder
- 4 eggs

Frosting:

- ½ cup crushed graham crackers
- 1 cup heavy cream
- 2 cups dark chocolate chips

Directions:

1. To make the cupcakes, combine the butter and sugar in a container until pale and creamy.
2. Put in the vanilla and eggs, one at a time and mix thoroughly.
3. Fold in the flours, graham crackers, salt, baking soda and cinnamon powder, alternating it with the milk.

4. Spoon the batter in a muffin tin coated with baking muffin papers.
5. Pre-heat the oven and bake at 350F for about twenty minutes or until the cupcakes pass the toothpick test.
6. Let cool in the pan.
7. To make the frosting, bring the cream to a boil in a saucepan. Turn off the heat and put in the chocolate. Stir until melted and smooth then let cool down.
8. Apply the frosting on top of each cupcake and drizzle with crushed graham crackers.

Nutritional Content of One Serving:
Calories: 421 Fat: 26.9g Protein: 5.8g Carbohydrates: 43.2g

Chocolate Malt Cupcakes

Total Time Taken: 1 hour
Yield: Servings 18
Ingredients:

Cupcakes:
- ¼ cup canola oil
- ½ teaspoon baking soda
- ½ teaspoon salt
- ¾ cups cocoa powder
- 1 cup malted milk powder
- 1 cup milk
- 1 cup sour cream
- 1 teaspoon baking powder
- 1 teaspoon vanilla extract
- 2 ¼ cups all-purpose flour
- 4 eggs

Frosting:
- ½ cup malted milk powder
- 1 ½ cups butter, softened
- 1 teaspoon vanilla extract
- 2 cups powdered sugar

Directions:
1. To make the cupcakes, combine the milk, milk powder, eggs, sour cream, vanilla and oil in a container.
2. Put in the flour, cocoa powder, salt, baking soda and baking powder and mix using a spatula.
3. Spoon the batter in a muffin tin covered with muffin papers.
4. Pre-heat the oven and bake at 350F for about twenty minutes or until a toothpick inserted into them comes out dry.
5. Let cool down before you serve.
6. To make the frosting, combine the butter in a container until airy.
7. Put in the milk powder and mix 2 minutes on high speed, then mix in the sugar and vanilla and continue mixing for five minutes on high speed.

8. Pipe the frosting on top of the cupcakes and serve them fresh.

Nutritional Content of One Serving:
Calories: 389 Fat: 23.6g Protein: 5.8g Carbohydrates: 41.3g

Chocolate Peanut Butter Cupcakes

Total Time Taken: 1 ½ hours
Yield: 12 Servings
Ingredients:
Cupcakes:
- ¼ cup smooth peanut butter
- ¼ teaspoon salt
- ½ cup butter, softened
- ½ cup sour cream
- 1 cup all-purpose flour
- 1 cup almond flour
- 1 teaspoon baking powder
- 1 teaspoon vanilla extract
- 2 eggs

Frosting:
- 1 cup heavy cream
- 1 teaspoon vanilla extract
- 2 cups dark chocolate chips

Directions:
1. To make the cupcakes, combine the butter and peanut butter in a container until creamy.
2. Put in the eggs and sour cream and mix thoroughly. Stir in the vanilla too.
3. Put in the flours, salt and baking powder and mix them using a spatula.
4. Spoon the batter in 12 muffin cups covered with muffin papers.
5. Preheat your oven and bake the cupcakes at 350F for about twenty minutes or until it rises significantly and seems golden.
6. Let them cool in the pan.
7. To make the frosting, bring the cream to a boil in a saucepan.
8. Turn off the heat and put in the chocolate chips. Stir until melted and smooth then allow to cool.
9. Spoon the frosting on top of each cupcake.

Nutritional Content of One Serving:
Calories: 312 Fat: 23.4g Protein: 5.8g Carbohydrates: 23.9g

Chocolate Pear Muffins

Total Time Taken: 1 hour
Yield: 12 Servings
Ingredients:
- ½ cup buttermilk

- ½ cup light brown sugar
- ½ cup milk
- ½ teaspoon salt
- 1 1/3 cups all-purpose flour
- 1 teaspoon baking powder
- 1/3 cup cocoa powder
- 2 eggs
- 2 pears, peeled and diced

Directions:
1. Mix the eggs, milk, sugar and buttermilk in a container.
2. Stir in the dry ingredients and stir for a few seconds to mix.
3. Fold in the pears then spoon the batter in a muffin tin covered with muffin papers.
4. Preheat your oven and bake the muffins at 350F for about twenty minutes or until well risen.
These muffins taste best chilled.

Nutritional Content of One Serving:
Calories: 119 Fat: 1.5g Protein: 3.6g Carbohydrates: 24.4g

Chocolate Pretzel Muffins

Total Time Taken: 1 ½ hours
Yield: 12 Servings
Ingredients:

Cupcakes:
- ¼ cup canola oil
- ¼ cup cocoa powder
- ¼ teaspoon salt
- ½ cup brewed coffee
- 1 ¼ cups all-purpose flour
- 1 ½ teaspoons baking powder
- 1 cup buttermilk
- 1 teaspoon vanilla extract
- 2 eggs

Frosting:
- ½ cup dark chocolate chips, melted and chilled
- 1 cup butter, softened
- 1 cup pretzels2 cups powdered sugar
- , crushed

Directions:
1. To make the cupcakes, combine the flour, cocoa powder, salt and baking powder in a container.
2. Put in the remaining ingredients and stir for a few seconds to mix.
3. Pour the batter in a muffin tin covered with muffin papers.

4. Pre-heat the oven and bake at 350F for about twenty minutes or until a toothpick inserted into the center of a muffin comes out clean.

5. Let cool down.

6. To make the frosting, combine the butter and sugar in a container until fluffy and pale.

7. Stir in the chocolate and mix thoroughly.

8. Top each cupcake with the frosting and drizzle with pretzels.

These cupcakes taste best when fresh.

Nutritional Content of One Serving:

Calories: 368 Fat: 22.6g Protein: 4.3g Carbohydrates: 39.5g

Chocolate Raspberry Crumble Muffins

Total Time Taken: 1 ¼ hours
Yield: 12 Servings
Ingredients:

Muffins:

- ¼ cup cocoa powder
- ½ cup butter, melted
- ½ cup milk
- ½ cup white sugar
- ½ teaspoon salt
- 1 ½ cups all-purpose flour
- 1 cup fresh raspberries
- 1 teaspoon vanilla extract
- 2 teaspoons baking powder
- 3 eggs

Crumble Topping:

- ¼ cup butter, chilled
- ¼ teaspoon salt
- ½ cup all-purpose flour

Directions:

1. For the muffins, combine the eggs, sugar and vanilla in a container until creamy.

2. Stir in the milk and butter and mix thoroughly.

3. Fold in the flour, cocoa powder, salt and baking powder then spoon the batter in a muffin pan coated with muffin papers.

4. For the topping, combine the ingredients in a container until grainy.

5. Top the muffins with the crumble topping and preheat your oven and bake at 350F for about twenty minutes or until well risen.

These muffins taste best chilled.

Nutritional Content of One Serving:

Calories: 241 Fat: 13.3g Protein: 4.4g Carbohydrates: 27.5g

Chocolate Raspberry Cupcakes

Total Time Taken: 1 ½ hours
Yield: 12 Servings
Ingredients:

Cupcakes:

- 2 eggs
- 1 teaspoon vanilla extract
- ¼ cup milk
- 1 ½ cups all-purpose flour
- ½ teaspoon salt
- 1 ½ teaspoons baking powder
- ¼ cup cocoa powder
- 2/3 cup butter, softened
- 2/3 cup white sugar

Frosting:

- ½ cup dark chocolate chips, melted and chilled
- 1 cup butter, softened
- 1 cup cream cheese
- 2 cups powdered sugar

Directions:

1. To make the cupcakes, combine the butter and sugar in a container until fluffy and airy.
2. Put in the eggs and vanilla and mix thoroughly. Stir in the milk.
3. Fold in the flour, salt, baking powder and cocoa and mix using a spatula.
4. Spoon the batter in a muffin tin covered with muffin papers and preheat your oven and bake at 350F for about twenty minutes or until well risen.
5. Let them cool in the pan.
6. For frosting, combine the cream cheese and butter in a container until pale.
7. Put in the sugar, progressively, and mix for five minutes on high speed.
8. Stir in the melted chocolate then spoon a dollop of frosting over each cupcake and serve fresh.

Nutritional Content of One Serving:
Calories: 512 Fat: 34.9g Protein: 5.1g Carbohydrates: 48.5g

Chocolate Spice Cupcakes

Total Time Taken: 1 ½ hours
Yield: 12 Servings
Ingredients:

Cupcakes:

- ¼ cup cocoa powder
- ½ cup white sugar
- ½ teaspoon cinnamon powder

- ½ teaspoon ground ginger
- ½ teaspoon ground star anise
- ½ teaspoon salt
- ¾ cup milk
- 1 ¼ cups all-purpose flour
- 1 ½ teaspoons baking powder
- 1 teaspoon vanilla extract
- 1/2 cup butter, softened
- 2 eggs

Frosting:
- ½ cup heavy cream
- 1 cup dark chocolate chips

Directions:
1. To make the cupcakes, combine the butter, sugar and vanilla in a container until fluffy and pale.
2. Put in the eggs and mix thoroughly then mix in the milk.
3. Fold in the flour, cocoa powder, salt, baking powder, cinnamon, ginger and star anise.
4. Spoon the batter in a muffin tin covered with muffin papers.
5. Preheat your oven and bake the cupcakes at 350F for about twenty minutes or until it rises completely and is aromatic.
6. Let the cupcakes cool down.
7. To make the frosting, bring the cream to a boil in a saucepan. Turn off the heat and mix in the chocolate chips. Stir until melted then spoon the frosting over each cupcake.
8. Serve immediately or store them in an airtight container.

Nutritional Content of One Serving:
Calories: 235 Fat: 13.6g Protein: 4.0g Carbohydrates: 27.4g

Chocolate Tahini Muffins

Total Time Taken: 1 hour
Yield: 12 Servings
Ingredients:
- ¼ cup cocoa powder
- ¼ cup light brown sugar
- ¼ cup maple syrup
- ¼ cup milk
- ¼ cup tahini paste
- ¼ teaspoon salt
- 1 ½ cups all-purpose flour
- 1 teaspoon baking powder
- 1 teaspoon vanilla extract
- 4 eggs

Directions:

1. Mix the eggs, tahini paste, maple syrup, sugar, vanilla and milk in a container.
2. Put in the flour, cocoa powder, salt and baking powder and stir for a few seconds to mix.
3. Spoon the batter in a muffin tin coated with baking muffin papers.
4. Pre-heat the oven and bake at 350F for about twenty minutes or until a toothpick inserted in the center of the muffins comes out clean.
5. Allow the muffins to cool to room temperature in the pan.

Nutritional Content of One Serving:

Calories: 144 Fat: 4.6g Protein: 4.8g Carbohydrates: 21.9g

Chunky Banana Muffins

Total Time Taken: 1 hour
Yield: 12 Servings
Ingredients:

- ¼ cup butter, melted
- ¼ teaspoon salt
- ½ cup cocoa powder
- ½ cup light brown sugar
- 1 ½ cups all-purpose flour
- 1 cup buttermilk
- 1 teaspoon vanilla extract
- 2 bananas, sliced
- 2 eggs
- 2 tablespoons molasses
- 2 teaspoons baking powder

Directions:

1. Mix the eggs and sugar in a container until pale and light. Put in the molasses and vanilla and mix thoroughly.
2. Stir in the butter and buttermilk then put in the flour, cocoa powder, salt and baking powder.
3. Fold in the banana slices and spoon the batter in a muffin tin lined using muffin papers of your choice.
4. Pre-heat the oven and bake at 350F for about twenty minutes. When finished, allow them to cool in the pan before you serve.

Nutritional Content of One Serving:

Calories: 169 Fat: 5.4g Protein: 4.1g Carbohydrates: 28.3g

Cinnamon Apple Cupcakes

Total Time Taken: 1 ½ hours
Yield: 12 Servings
Ingredients:

Cupcakes:

- ¼ cup milk
- ½ cup butter, softened
- ½ cup light brown sugar

- ½ teaspoon salt
- 1 ½ cups all-purpose flour
- 1 teaspoon baking powder
- 1 teaspoon grated ginger
- 1 teaspoon vanilla extract
- 2 red apples, cored and diced
- 3 eggs

Frosting:
- 1 cup butter, softened
- 1 teaspoon cinnamon powder
- 1 teaspoon vanilla extract
- 2 cups powdered sugar

Directions:
1. To make the cupcakes, combine the butter and sugar in a container until fluffy and creamy.
2. Put in the eggs, one at a time, and mix thoroughly then mix in the vanilla and ginger.
3. Fold in the flour, salt and baking powder, alternating it with milk. Fold in the apples.
4. Spoon the batter in a muffin tin covered with muffin papers.
5. Preheat your oven and bake the cupcakes at 350F for about twenty minutes. Let the cupcakes cool in the pan.
6. To make the frosting, combine the butter in a container until fluffy. Put in the sugar and mix thoroughly then mix in the cinnamon and vanilla. Whip on high speed for five minutes.
7. Top each cupcake with the frosting and serve them fresh.

Nutritional Content of One Serving:
Calories: 398 Fat: 24.4g Protein: 3.5g Carbohydrates: 42.7g

Cinnamon Autumn Muffins

Total Time Taken: 1 hour
Yield: 12 Servings
Ingredients:
- ½ cup butter, melted
- ½ cup butternut squash cubes
- ½ cup milk
- ½ teaspoon salt
- 1 apple, cored and diced
- 1 pear, cored and diced
- 1 teaspoon cinnamon powder
- 1 teaspoon vanilla extract
- 2 cups all-purpose flour
- 2 eggs
- 2 teaspoons baking powder
- 2/3 cup light brown sugar

Directions:

1. Mix the flour, salt, baking powder, cinnamon and sugar in a container.
2. Put in the butter, eggs, milk and vanilla and mix thoroughly.
3. Fold in the apple, pear and butternut squash cubes.
4. Spoon the batter in a muffin tin coated with baking muffin papers.
5. Pre-heat the oven and bake at 350F for about twenty minutes or until it rises significantly and seems golden.

These muffins taste best chilled.

Nutritional Content of One Serving:

Calories: 208 Fat: 8.9g Protein: 3.6g Carbohydrates: 29.1g

Cinnamon Blueberry Muffins

Total Time Taken: 1 hour
Yield: 12 Servings
Ingredients:

- ½ cup butter, melted
- ½ cup light brown sugar
- ½ cup milk
- ½ teaspoon cinnamon powder
- ½ teaspoon salt
- 1 cup blueberries
- 1 teaspoon baking soda
- 2 cups all-purpose flour
- 2 eggs

Directions:

1. Mix the flour, sugar, salt, baking soda and cinnamon in a container.
2. Put in the milk, eggs and melted butter and fold in the blueberries then spoon the batter in a muffin tin covered with muffin papers.
3. Preheat your oven and bake the muffins at 350F for about twenty minutes or until it rises significantly and starts to appear golden-brown.

These muffins taste best chilled.

Nutritional Content of One Serving:

Calories: 189 Fat: 8.8g Protein: 3.6g Carbohydrates: 24.1g

Cinnamon Plum Muffins

Total Time Taken: 1 hour
Yield: 12 Servings
Ingredients:

- ¼ cup canola oil
- ½ cup ground walnuts
- ½ cup light brown sugar
- ½ teaspoon ground ginger

- 1 ½ cups all-purpose flour
- 1 cup buttermilk
- 1 egg
- 1 teaspoon baking soda
- 1 teaspoon cinnamon powder
- 1 teaspoon vanilla extract
- 6 plums, pitted and diced

Directions:

1. Mix the flour, sugar, baking soda, cinnamon, ginger and walnuts in a container.
2. Put in the remaining ingredients and mix thoroughly. Put in the plums as well.
3. Spoon the batter in a muffin tin lined using muffin papers of your choice.
4. Pre-heat the oven and bake at 350F for about twenty minutes or until it rises significantly and starts to appear golden-brown.

These muffins taste best chilled.

Nutritional Content of One Serving:

Calories: 177 Fat: 8.4g Protein: 4.2g Carbohydrates: 22.0g

Citrus Coconut Muffins

Total Time Taken: 1 hour
Yield: 12 Servings
Ingredients:

- ¼ cup milk
- ½ cup butter, melted
- ½ cup white sugar
- ½ teaspoon salt
- 1 cup coconut flakes
- 1 teaspoon lemon zest
- 1 teaspoon lime zest
- 1 teaspoon orange zest
- 2 cups all-purpose flour
- 2 eggs
- 2 teaspoons baking powder

Directions:

1. Mix the eggs and sugar in a container until pale and light. Put in the melted butter and citrus zest and mix thoroughly.
2. Fold in the dry ingredients, as well as the coconut flakes then spoon the batter in 12 muffin cups covered with muffin papers.
3. Preheat your oven and bake the muffins at 350F for about twenty minutes or until a golden-brown colour is achieved and it rises significantly.
4. Let cool in the pan before you serve.

Nutritional Content of One Serving:

Calories: 213 Fat: 10.9g Protein: 3.5g Carbohydrates: 26.1g

Citrus Iced Coconut Cupcakes

Total Time Taken: 1 ¼ hours
Yield: 12 Servings
Ingredients:

Cupcakes:

- ¼ teaspoon salt
- ½ cup coconut butter
- ½ cup coconut flakes
- ½ cup coconut milk
- ½ cup white sugar
- 1 ½ cups all-purpose flour
- 1 ½ teaspoons baking powder
- 2 eggs

Icing:

- 1 ½ cups powdered sugar
- 1 tablespoon lime juice
- 1 teaspoon lemon zest
- 1 teaspoon lime zest

Directions:

1. To make the cupcakes, combine the coconut butter and sugar until creamy.
2. Put in the eggs, one at a time, then mix in the coconut milk.
3. Fold in the flour, coconut flakes, salt and baking powder then spoon the batter in a muffin tin covered with muffin papers.
4. Preheat your oven and bake the muffins at 350F for about twenty minutes or until a golden-brown colour is achieved and it rises significantly. Let them cool in the pan.
5. For the icing, combine all the ingredients in a container.
6. Sprinkle the icing over each cupcake and serve them fresh.

Nutritional Content of One Serving:

Calories: 212 Fat: 6.2g Protein: 3.1g Carbohydrates: 37.7g

Coconut Caramel Cupcakes

Total Time Taken: 1 ½ hours
Yield: 14 Servings
Ingredients:

Cupcakes:

- ½ cup butter, softened
- ½ cup coconut cream
- ½ cup coconut milk
- ½ teaspoon salt

- 1 ½ cups all-purpose flour
- 1 cup white sugar
- 1 teaspoon vanilla extract
- 2 teaspoons baking powder
- 2/3 cup shredded coconut
- 3 eggs

Frosting:
- ½ cup caramel sauce
- 1 cup butter, softened
- 1 cup coconut flakes
- 1 teaspoon vanilla extract
- 2 cups powdered sugar

Directions:
1. To make the cupcakes, combine the butter and sugar in a container until fluffy and pale.
2. Put in the eggs and mix thoroughly then mix in the coconut cream, milk and vanilla.
3. Fold in the flour, coconut, salt and baking powder.
4. Spoon the batter in a muffin tin covered with muffin papers and preheat your oven and bake at 350F for about twenty minutes or until a golden-brown colour is achieved and it rises significantly.
5. Let the cupcakes cool down.
6. To make the frosting, combine the butter and sugar in a container for about five to seven minutes or until fluffy and pale.
7. Put in the vanilla and mix thoroughly. Top each cupcake with the frosting then garnish with coconut flakes.
8. Just before you serve, sprinkle the cupcakes with caramel sauce.

Nutritional Content of One Serving:
Calories: 462 Fat: 28.1g Protein: 3.7g Carbohydrates: 52.2g

Coconut Cupcakes

Total Time Taken: 1 ½ hours
Yield: 12 Servings
Ingredients:

Cupcakes:
- ½ cup butter, softened
- ½ cup shredded coconut
- ½ teaspoon salt
- ¾ cup coconut milk
- ¾ cup white sugar
- 1 ½ teaspoons baking powder
- 1 ¾ cup all-purpose flour
- 1 teaspoon vanilla extract
- 3 eggs

Frosting:

- ½ cup butter, softened
- ½ cup cream cheese, softened
- 1 teaspoon vanilla extract
- 2 cups powdered sugar

Directions:

1. To make the cupcakes, combine the butter, sugar and vanilla in a container until fluffy and pale.
2. Put in the eggs, one at a time, then fold in the flour, baking powder, salt and coconut, alternating it with milk. Begin with flour and finish with flour.
3. Spoon the batter in 12 muffin cups covered with muffin papers.
4. Pre-heat the oven and bake at 350F for about twenty minutes or until it rises significantly and starts to appear golden-brown.
5. Let the cupcakes cool in the pan.
6. To make the frosting, combine the butter, cream cheese and sugar in a container for five minutes or until fluffy and pale.
7. Stir in the vanilla and mix thoroughly then spoon the frosting in a pastry bag and top the cupcakes with it.

Nutritional Content of One Serving:

Calories: 425 Fat: 24.7g Protein: 4.6g Carbohydrates: 48.4g

Coconut Flakes Cupcakes

Total Time Taken: 1 ½ hours
Yield: 12 Servings
Ingredients:

Cupcakes:

- ¼ teaspoon salt
- ½ cup butter, softened
- ½ cup white sugar
- 1 cup all-purpose flour
- 1 cup shredded coconut
- 1 teaspoon baking powder
- 1 teaspoon coconut extract
- 3 eggs

Frosting:

- 1 cup butter, softened
- 1 cup coconut flakes
- 2 cups powdered sugar

Directions:

1. To make the cupcakes, combine the butter and sugar in a container until pale and light.
2. Put in the coconut extract and eggs and mix thoroughly.
3. Fold in the flour, salt, baking powder and shredded coconut.

4. Spoon the batter in a muffin tin covered with muffin papers.

5. Preheat your oven and bake the cupcakes at 350F for about twenty minutes or until it rises significantly and seems golden. Let the cupcakes cool down.

6. To make the frosting, combine the butter until pale. Put in the sugar and stir thoroughly for five minutes.

7. Spoon the frosting in a pastry bag and top each cupcake with it.

8. Garnish the frosted cupcakes with coconut flakes.

These cupcakes taste best when fresh.

Nutritional Content of One Serving:

Calories: 415 Fat: 28.7g Protein: 3.2g Carbohydrates: 38.6g

Coconut Lemon Chia Seed Muffins

Total Time Taken: 1 hour
Yield: 10 Servings
Ingredients:

- ¼ cup coconut oil, melted
- ¼ teaspoon salt
- ½ cup honey
- ½ cup milk
- 1 ½ cups almond flour
- 1 teaspoon baking powder
- 1 teaspoon lemon juice
- 1 teaspoon lemon zest
- 1 teaspoon vanilla extract
- 2 tablespoons chia seeds
- 4 eggs

Directions:

1. Mix the chia seeds, almond flour, salt and baking powder in a container.

2. Put in the remaining ingredients and stir for a few seconds to mix.

3. Pour the batter in a muffin tin covered with muffin papers.

4. Pre-heat the oven and bake at 350F for about twenty minutes or until it rises significantly and seems golden.

5. Let the muffins cool in the pan before you serve.

Nutritional Content of One Serving:

Calories: 187 Fat: 11.5g Protein: 4.8g Carbohydrates: 18.0g

Coconut Mango Muffins

Total Time Taken: 1 hour
Yield: 12 Servings
Ingredients:

- ½ cup canola oil
- ½ cup coconut milk

- ½ cup white sugar
- ½ teaspoon salt
- 1 ½ teaspoons baking powder
- 1 cup all-purpose flour
- 1 cup shredded coconut
- 1 mango, peeled and diced
- 1 teaspoon vanilla extract
- 2 eggs

Directions:

1. Mix the oil, eggs, sugar, vanilla and coconut milk in a container.
2. Put in the coconut, flour, salt and baking powder then fold in the mango.
3. Spoon the batter in a muffin tin covered with muffin papers or greased and preheat your oven and bake at 350F for about twenty minutes or until it rises significantly and starts to appear golden-brown.

These muffins taste best chilled.

Nutritional Content of One Serving:

Calories: 220 Fat: 14.6g Protein: 2.5g Carbohydrates: 21.2g

Coconut Muffins

Total Time Taken: 1 hour
Yield: 12 Servings
Ingredients:

- ½ cup canola oil
- ½ cup light brown sugar
- ½ cup quinoa flour
- ½ cup raspberry jam
- ½ cup shredded coconut
- ½ teaspoon salt
- 1 ½ cups all-purpose flour
- 1 egg
- 1 teaspoon baking soda
- 1 teaspoon vanilla extract
- 2/3 cup milk

Directions:

1. Mix the flours, baking soda, salt, coconut and sugar.
2. Stir in the egg, milk, oil and vanilla and stir for a few seconds to mix using a spatula.
3. Spoon the batter in a muffin tin covered with muffin papers.
4. Drop a dollop of raspberry jam on top of each muffin and preheat your oven and bake at 350F for about twenty minutes or until it rises significantly and starts to appear golden-brown.

These muffins taste best chilled.

Nutritional Content of One Serving:

Calories: 237 Fat: 11.5g Protein: 4.4g Carbohydrates: 28.9g

White Chocolate Pumpkin Cupcakes

Total Time Taken: 1 ½ hours
Yield: 14 Servings
Ingredients:

Cupcakes:

- ¼ cup canola oil
- ½ cup dark chocolate chips
- ½ cup light brown sugar
- ½ cup milk
- ½ teaspoon baking soda
- ½ teaspoon cinnamon powder
- ½ teaspoon ground cardamom
- ½ teaspoon ground ginger
- ½ teaspoon salt
- 1 cup pumpkin puree
- 1 teaspoon baking powder
- 1 teaspoon vanilla extract
- 2 cups all-purpose flour
- 2 eggs

Frosting:

- 1 cup heavy cream
- 1 teaspoon vanilla extract
- 2 cups white chocolate chips
- 2 tablespoons butter

Directions:

1. To make the cupcakes, combine the flour, baking powder, baking soda, spices and salt in a container.
2. Mix the eggs and sugar in a container until fluffy and pale.
3. Put in the milk, pumpkin puree, canola oil and vanilla and mix thoroughly.
4. Fold in the flour mixture then spoon the batter in a muffin tin covered with muffin papers.
5. Pre-heat the oven and bake at 350F for about twenty minutes or until the cupcakes pass the toothpick test.
6. Let them cool in the pan.
7. To make the frosting, bring the cream to a boil. Turn off the heat and mix in the chocolate. Stir until melted and smooth.
8. Put in the vanilla and butter and mix thoroughly.
9. Let cool completely then whip the cream until fluffy and pale.
10. Top the cupcakes with the frosting and garnish with a dusting of cinnamon powder.

Nutritional Content of One Serving:

Calories: 336 Fat: 18.7g Protein: 5.1g Carbohydrates: 38.4g

White Chocolate Pumpkin Cupcakes

Total Time Taken: 1 ½ hours
Yield: 12 Servings
Ingredients:

Cupcakes:

- ¼ teaspoon ground cardamom
- ¼ teaspoon salt
- ½ cup butter, softened
- ½ cup buttermilk
- ½ teaspoon ground ginger
- 1 ½ cups all-purpose flour
- 1 cup pumpkin puree
- 1 teaspoon cinnamon powder
- 2 eggs
- 2 tablespoons canola oil
- 2/3 cup light brown sugar

Frosting:

- 1 cup heavy cream
- 2 cups white chocolate chips

Directions:

1. To make the cupcakes, combine the butter, oil and sugar in a container until fluffy and pale.
2. Put in the eggs and mix thoroughly then mix in the pumpkin puree and buttermilk.
3. Fold in the remaining ingredients then spoon the batter in a muffin tin covered with muffin papers.
4. Pre-heat the oven and bake at 350F for about twenty minutes or until it rises significantly and becomes aromatic.
5. Let cool in the pan completely.
6. To make the frosting, bring the cream to a boil in a saucepan. Turn off the heat and put in the chocolate. Stir until melted then let cool down.
7. Pipe the frosting over each cupcake and serve them fresh.

Nutritional Content of One Serving:
Calories: 385 Fat: 23.8g Protein: 5.1g Carbohydrates: 39.2g

Whole Wheat Banana Muffins

Total Time Taken: 1 hour
Yield: 12 Servings
Ingredients:

- ¼ cup canola oil
- ¼ teaspoon cinnamon powder
- ¼ teaspoon salt
- ½ cup light brown sugar

- 1 cup buttermilk
- 2 bananas, mashed
- 2 cups whole wheat flour
- 2 eggs
- 2 teaspoons baking powder

Directions:

1. Mix the dry ingredients in a container.
2. Put in the remaining ingredients, all at once, and stir for a few seconds to mix with a whisk.
3. Pour the batter in a muffin tin coated with baking muffin papers and preheat your oven and bake at 350F for about twenty minutes or until a toothpick inserted into them comes out dry.
4. *Let cool down before you serve.*

Nutritional Content of One Serving:

Calories: 176 Fat: 5.7g Protein: 4.0g Carbohydrates: 27.7g

Whole Wheat Strawberry Muffins

Total Time Taken: 1 hour
Yield: 12 Servings
Ingredients:

- 2 eggs
- 2 cups whole wheat flour
- 2 bananas, mashed
- 1 teaspoon vanilla extract
- 1 teaspoon baking soda
- 1 teaspoon baking powder
- 1 cup strawberries, sliced
- ½ cup light brown sugar
- ½ cup canola oil
- ½ cup applesauce

Directions:

1. Mix the eggs, applesauce, canola oil, bananas, sugar and vanilla in a container.
2. Put in the flour, baking soda and baking powder and stir swiftly to combine.
3. Fold in the strawberries then spoon the batter in a muffin tin coated with baking muffin papers.
4. Preheat your oven and bake the muffins at 350F for about twenty minutes or until a toothpick inserted into them comes out dry.

These muffins taste best chilled.

Nutritional Content of One Serving:

Calories: 217 Fat: 10.1g Protein: 3.4g Carbohydrates: 28.7g

Wholemeal Muffins

Total Time Taken: 1 hour
Yield: 12 Servings
Ingredients:

- ¼ cup canola oil
- ½ cup white sugar
- ½ cup whole wheat flour
- ½ teaspoon salt
- 1 ½ cups all-purpose flour
- 1 cup milk
- 1 egg
- 2 tablespoons chia seeds
- 2 tablespoons hemp seeds
- 2 teaspoons baking powder

Directions:

1. Mix the flour, wheat flour, baking powder, salt, chia seeds and hemp seeds.
2. Put in the sugar, egg, milk and canola oil and stir for a few seconds to mix.
3. Spoon the batter into a muffin tin covered with muffin papers and preheat your oven and bake at 350F for about twenty minutes or until a golden-brown colour is achieved and it rises significantly.

These muffins taste best chilled.

Nutritional Content of One Serving:

Calories: 182 Fat: 6.9g Protein: 4.2g Carbohydrates: 25.9g

Wholesome Blueberry Muffins

Total Time Taken: 1 hour
Yield: 12 Servings
Ingredients:

- ¼ cup wheat bran
- ½ cup butter, melted
- ½ cup milk
- ½ teaspoon salt
- 1 cup all-purpose flour
- 1 cup fresh blueberries
- 1 cup whole wheat flour
- 2 eggs
- 2 tablespoons orange marmalade
- 2 teaspoons baking powder

Directions:

1. Mix the flours, bran, baking powder and salt in a container.
2. Put in the butter, eggs, milk and marmalade then fold in blueberries.

3. Spoon the batter in a muffin tin covered with muffin papers and preheat your oven and bake at 350F for about twenty minutes or until it rises significantly and starts to appear golden-brown.

These muffins taste best chilled.

Nutritional Content of One Serving:
Calories: 213 Fat: 10.7g Protein: 4.5g Carbohydrates: 25.9g

Yogurt Blackberry Muffins

Total Time Taken: 1 hour
Yield: 12 Servings
Ingredients:

- ¼ teaspoon salt
- ½ cup butter, melted
- ½ cup heavy cream
- 1 cup blackberries
- 1 cup white sugar
- 1 teaspoon vanilla extract
- 2 cups all-purpose flour
- 2 egg whites
- 2 eggs
- 2 teaspoons baking powder

Directions:

1. Mix the flour, baking powder and salt in a container.
2. Whip the eggs, egg whites, vanilla and sugar until fluffy and pale.
3. Put in the butter and mix thoroughly then mix in the cream.
4. Fold in the flour then put in the blackberries.
5. Spoon the batter in a muffin tin covered with muffin papers.
6. Pre-heat the oven and bake at 350F for about twenty minutes or until it rises significantly and starts to appear golden-brown.
7. Let the muffins cool to room temperature before you serve.

Nutritional Content of One Serving:
Calories: 244 Fat: 10.5g Protein: 4.0g Carbohydrates: 34.4g

Yogurt Vanilla Berry Muffins

Total Time Taken: 1 hour
Yield: 12 Servings
Ingredients:

- ¼ cup canola oil
- ¼ teaspoon salt
- ½ teaspoon baking soda
- 1 ¾ cups all-purpose flour
- 1 cup Greek yogurt

- 1 cup mixed berries
- 1 tablespoon vanilla extract
- 1 teaspoon baking powder
- 2 eggs

Directions:

1. Mix the eggs, oil, yogurt and vanilla in a container.
2. Put in the flour, salt, baking powder and baking soda and stir for a few seconds to mix just until incorporated.
3. Fold in the berries then spoon the batter in a muffin tin covered with muffin papers.
4. Pre-heat the oven and bake at 350F for about twenty minutes or until a toothpick inserted into them comes out dry.
5. Let cool in the pan before you serve.

Nutritional Content of One Serving:

Calories: 140 Fat: 5.8g Protein: 4.6g Carbohydrates: 16.4g

Zesty Pistachio Muffins

Total Time Taken: 1 hour
Yield: 12 Servings
Ingredients:

- ¼ cup canola oil
- ¼ cup plain yogurt
- ¼ teaspoon salt
- 1 cup all-purpose flour
- 1 cup fresh raspberries
- 1 cup ground pistachio
- 1 cup white sugar
- 1 teaspoon baking powder
- 1 teaspoon vanilla extract
- 3 eggs

Directions:

1. Mix the eggs and sugar in a container until volume increases to twice what it was.
2. Put in the oil, vanilla and yogurt and mix thoroughly.
3. Fold in the remaining ingredients then spoon the batter in a muffin tin covered with muffin papers.
4. Preheat your oven and bake the muffins at 350F for about twenty minutes or until it rises significantly and starts to appear golden-brown.
5. Let cool in the pan before you serve.

Nutritional Content of One Serving:

Calories: 184 Fat: 6.7g Protein: 3.3g Carbohydrates: 28.8g

Zucchini Carrot Muffins

Total Time Taken: 1 hour
Yield: 12 Servings
Ingredients:

- ¼ cup maple syrup
- ¼ teaspoon salt
- ½ cup brown rice flour
- ½ cup canola oil
- ½ cup golden raisins
- ½ teaspoon cinnamon powder
- 1 ½ teaspoons baking powder
- 1 cup almond flour
- 1 cup grated carrots
- 1 cup grated zucchinis
- 1 egg

Directions:

1. Mix the flours, salt, baking powder and cinnamon in a container.
2. Stir in the canola oil, maple syrup and egg and stir for a few seconds to mix.
3. Fold in the carrots, zucchinis and raisins then spoon the batter in a muffin tin covered with muffin papers.
4. Pre-heat the oven and bake at 350F for about twenty minutes or until a toothpick inserted into them comes out dry.

These muffins taste best chilled.

Nutritional Content of One Serving:
Calories: 164 Fat: 10.8g Protein: 1.8g Carbohydrates: 16.3g

Zucchini Chocolate Muffins

Total Time Taken: 1 hour
Yield: 12 Servings
Ingredients:

- 1 teaspoon baking soda
- 1 egg
- 1 cup grated zucchinis
- 1 ½ cups all-purpose flour
- ¾ cup white sugar
- ½ teaspoon salt
- ½ teaspoon cinnamon powder
- ½ cup walnuts, chopped
- ½ cup cocoa powder
- ½ cup canola oil

- ¼ cup buttermilk

Directions:

1. Mix the flour, cocoa powder, sugar, baking soda, cinnamon and salt in a container.
2. Stir in the egg, canola oil, buttermilk and zucchinis then fold in the walnuts.
3. Pour the batter in a muffin tin lined using muffin papers of your choice and preheat your oven and bake at 350F for about twenty minutes or until it rises significantly and becomes aromatic.
4. Let the muffins cool in the pan before you serve.

Nutritional Content of One Serving:

Calories: 233 Fat: 13.2g Protein: 4.2g Carbohydrates: 27.5g

Anna Goldman is an American professional baker. Born and raised in Kentucky, Anna loved her mother's baking and gradually developed an affinity to it. She started baking with her mother's recipes, and eventually came up with recipes of her own. She had always wanted to write a book about baking, but never got the time to do so until she had to shut down her bakery temporarily due to the coronavirus. Every cloud has a silver lining!

Almond Vanilla Cupcakes

Total Time Taken: 1 ½ hours
Yield: 12 Servings
Ingredients:

Cupcakes:

- ¼ cup milk
- ½ cup butter, softened
- ½ cup white sugar
- ½ teaspoon salt
- 1 cup all-purpose flour
- 1 cup ground almonds
- 1 teaspoon baking powder
- 1 teaspoon lemon zest
- 1 teaspoon vanilla extract
- 2 eggs

Glaze:

- 1 cup powdered sugar
- 1 tablespoon butter, melted
- 1 teaspoon lemon zest

Directions:

1. To make the cupcakes, combine the butter, sugar and vanilla in a container until fluffy and pale.
2. Put in the eggs, one at a time, then mix in the lemon zest and put in the flour, almonds, salt and baking powder.
3. Stir in the milk and mix for a minute on high speed.
4. Spoon the batter in a muffin tin covered with muffin papers and preheat your oven and bake at 350F for about twenty minutes or until a golden-brown colour is achieved and it rises significantly.
5. Let the cupcakes cool in the pan.

6. For the glaze, combine all the ingredients in a container. Sprinkle the glaze over each cupcake and serve fresh.

Nutritional Content of One Serving:
Calories: 245 Fat: 13.5g Protein: 3.9g Carbohydrates: 28.6g

Almond Vanilla Cupcakes

Total Time Taken: 1 ½ hours
Yield: 12 Servings
Ingredients:
Cupcakes:
- ½ cup all-purpose flour
- ½ cup butter, softened
- ½ cup buttermilk
- ½ cup white sugar
- ½ teaspoon almond extract
- ½ teaspoon salt
- 1 ½ cups almond flour
- 1 teaspoon baking soda
- 1 teaspoon vanilla extract
- 2 eggs

Frosting:
- 1 cup butter, softened
- 1 tablespoon vanilla extract
- 2 cups powdered sugar

Directions:
1. To make the cupcakes, combine the flours, salt and baking soda in a container.
2. In a separate container, combine the butter, sugar and vanilla until fluffy and creamy.
3. Put in the eggs, one at a time, then mix in the buttermilk and almond extract.
4. Fold in the flour mixture then spoon the batter in a muffin tin covered with muffin papers.
5. Pre-heat the oven and bake at 350F for about twenty minutes or until a golden-brown colour is achieved.
6. Let them cool in the pan.
7. To make the frosting, combine the butter and sugar for five minutes until pale and fluffy.
8. Put in the vanilla and mix thoroughly.
9. Spoon the frosting in a pastry bag and top the cupcakes with it.

Nutritional Content of One Serving:
Calories: 371 Fat: 25.7g Protein: 2.8g Carbohydrates: 33.8g

Almond White Chocolate Cupcakes

Total Time Taken: 1 ½ hours
Yield: 12 Servings
Ingredients:

Cupcakes:

- ½ cup all-purpose flour
- ½ cup butter, softened
- ½ cup plain yogurt
- ½ teaspoon almond extract
- ½ teaspoon salt
- ¾ cup white sugar
- 1 ½ teaspoons baking powder
- 1 cup almond flour
- 1 teaspoon vanilla extract
- 3 eggs

Frosting:

- 1 cup heavy cream
- 2 cups white chocolate chips

Directions:

1. To make the cupcakes, combine the butter and sugar in a container until fluffy and pale.
2. Put in the vanilla, almond extract and eggs and mix thoroughly.
3. Stir in the yogurt and stir thoroughly until blended.
4. Fold in the flours, salt, baking powder and mix using a spatula.
5. Spoon the batter in a muffin tin covered with muffin papers and preheat your oven and bake at 350F for about twenty minutes or until it rises significantly and seems golden.
6. Let them cool in the pan.
7. To make the frosting, bring the cream to a boil then remove from the
8. heat and put in the chocolate. Stir until melted and smooth then let cool in your refrigerator for a few hours.
9. When chilled, whip the frosting until airy and fluffy. Spoon the frosting in a pastry bag and top the cupcakes with it.
   10. *Serve immediately.*

Nutritional Content of One Serving:
Calories: 359 Fat: 22.9g Protein: 5.0g Carbohydrates: 35.2g

Apple Cranberry Muffins

Total Time Taken: 1 hour
Yield: 12 Servings
Ingredients:

- ¼ teaspoon salt
- ½ cup butter, melted
- ½ cup dried cranberries
- ½ cup light brown sugar
- ½ cup milk
- ½ teaspoon cinnamon powder

- 1 ¾ cups all-purpose flour
- 1 egg
- 1 red apple, cored and diced
- 1 teaspoon baking soda
- 1 teaspoon vanilla extract

Directions:

1. Mix the flour, sugar, baking soda, salt and cinnamon in a container.
2. Stir in the butter, milk, egg and vanilla and stir for a few seconds to mix.
3. Fold in the apple and cranberries and spoon the batter in a muffin tin lined using muffin papers of your choice.
4. Preheat your oven and bake the muffins at 350F for about twenty minutes or until it rises significantly and seems golden.

These muffins taste best chilled.

Nutritional Content of One Serving:

Calories: 179 Fat: 8.4g Protein: 2.8g Carbohydrates: 22.9g

Apple Muffins

Total Time Taken: 1 hour
Yield: 12 Servings
Ingredients:

- ¼ cup canola oil
- ½ cup ground walnuts
- ½ cup plain yogurt
- ½ cup white sugar
- ½ cup whole wheat flour
- ½ teaspoon cinnamon powder
- ½ teaspoon salt
- 1 cup all-purpose flour
- 1 teaspoon baking soda
- 1 teaspoon vanilla extract
- 2 apples, peeled, cored and diced
- 2 eggs

Directions:

1. Mix the eggs and sugar until fluffy and pale.
2. Put in the vanilla, oil and yogurt and stir thoroughly until blended.
3. Fold in the flour mixture then put in the apples.
4. Spoon the batter in a muffin tin covered with muffin papers and preheat your oven and bake at 350F for about twenty minutes or until a golden-brown colour is achieved and it rises significantly.

These muffins taste best chilled.

Nutritional Content of One Serving:

Calories: 195 Fat: 8.7g Protein: 4.5g Carbohydrates: 25.8g

Apple Pie Caramel Cupcakes

Total Time Taken: 1 ½ hours
Yield: 14 Servings

Ingredients:

- ½ teaspoon baking soda
- ½ teaspoon ground ginger
- 1 ½ cups all-purpose flour
- 1 pinch salt
- 1 teaspoon baking powder
- 1 teaspoon vanilla extract
- 2 eggs
- 2/3 cup butter, softened
- 2/3 cup buttermilk
- 2/3 cup light brown sugar

Frosting:

- ½ teaspoon cinnamon powder
- 1 cup butter, softened
- 2 cups powdered sugar

Topping:

- ¼ cup light brown sugar
- 1 tablespoon lemon juice
- 2 apples, peeled, cored and diced

Directions:

1. To make the cupcakes, combine the butter and sugar in a container until creamy and fluffy.
2. Put in the eggs and vanilla and mix thoroughly then mix in the buttermilk.
3. Put in the flour, spices, baking powder, baking soda and salt then pour the batter in a muffin tin covered with muffin papers.
4. Pre-heat the oven and bake at 350F for about twenty minutes or until a toothpick inserted into them comes out dry.
5. To make the frosting, combine the butter and sugar in a container for five minutes until pale and airy. Put in the cinnamon and mix thoroughly.
6. Top each cupcake with the frosting.
7. For the topping, mix the ingredients in a saucepan and cook over low heat just until the apples are tender. Let cool down then top each cupcake with a spoonfuls of apple mixture.

These cupcakes taste best when fresh.

Nutritional Content of One Serving:

Calories: 374 Fat: 22.9g Protein: 2.9g Carbohydrates: 41.1g

Apple Puree Muffins

Total Time Taken: 1 hour
Yield: 12 Servings
Ingredients:

- 1 ½ cups all-purpose flour
- 1 teaspoon cinnamon powder
- ½ teaspoon ground ginger
- 1 teaspoon baking soda
- 2 eggs
- ½ cup apple puree
- ¼ cup peanut oil
- 1 teaspoon vanilla extract
- 2 apples, cored and diced
- ½ cup golden raisins
- 2/3 cup light brown sugar

Directions:

1. Mix the flour, sugar, cinnamon, ginger and baking soda in a container.
2. Put in the remaining ingredients and stir for a few seconds to mix.
3. Pour the batter in a muffin tin coated with baking muffin papers.
4. Preheat your oven and bake the muffins at 350F for about twenty minutes or until it is aromatic and appears golden brown.

These muffins taste best chilled.

Nutritional Content of One Serving:
Calories: 179 Fat: 5.5g Protein: 2.8g Carbohydrates: 30.4g

Apricot Orange Muffins

Total Time Taken: 1 hour
Yield: 12 Servings
Ingredients:

- ¼ cup wheat bran
- ¼ teaspoon orange juice
- ½ cup buttermilk
- ½ cup canola oil
- ½ cup light brown sugar
- ½ teaspoon salt
- 1 ½ cups all-purpose flour
- 1 ½ teaspoons baking powder
- 1 tablespoon orange zest
- 2 eggs
- 6 apricots, halved

Directions:

1. Mix the flour, wheat bran, salt and baking powder in a container.
2. Put in the eggs, sugar, buttermilk, orange zest and orange juice and stir for a few seconds to mix.
3. Spoon the batter in a muffin tin covered with muffin papers.
4. Top each muffin with one apricot half and preheat your oven and bake at 350F for about twenty minutes or until a golden-brown colour is achieved and it rises significantly.

These muffins taste best chilled.

Nutritional Content of One Serving:

Calories: 187 Fat: 10.2g Protein: 3.3g Carbohydrates: 21.5g

Apricot Rosemary Muffins

Total Time Taken: 1 hour
Yield: 12 Servings
Ingredients:

- ¼ cup milk
- ¼ teaspoon salt
- ½ cup dried apricots, chopped
- ½ cup ground almonds
- ½ cup honey
- ½ cup plain yogurt
- ½ cup rolled oats
- 1 ½ cups all-purpose flour
- 1 egg
- 1 teaspoon baking powder
- 1 teaspoon dried rosemary

Directions:

1. Mix the flour, salt, baking powder, oats, almonds and rosemary in a container.
2. Stir in the honey, yogurt, milk and egg and mix thoroughly then fold in the apricots.
3. Spoon the batter in a muffin pan coated with your favorite muffin papers and preheat your oven and bake at 350F for about twenty minutes or until it rises significantly and starts to appear golden-brown.

These muffins taste best chilled.

Nutritional Content of One Serving:

Calories: 155 Fat: 3.0g Protein: 4.2g Carbohydrates: 28.7g

Banana Buttermilk Muffins

Total Time Taken: 1 hour
Yield: 12 Servings
Ingredients:

- ¼ cup butter, melted
- ½ cup rolled oats
- ½ cup white sugar

- ½ teaspoon salt
- 1 ¾ cups all-purpose flour
- 1 cup buttermilk
- 1 egg
- 1 teaspoon baking powder
- 1 teaspoon baking soda
- 2 ripe bananas, mashed

Directions:

1. Mix the dry ingredients in a container and the wet ingredients in a separate container.
2. Pour the wet ingredients over the dry ones and stir swiftly to combine.
3. Spoon the batter in a muffin pan coated with muffin papers.
4. Preheat your oven and bake the muffins at 350F for about twenty minutes or until a golden-brown colour is achieved or until mildly golden-brown and it rises significantly.

These muffins taste best chilled.

Nutritional Content of One Serving:

Calories: 176 Fat: 4.8g Protein: 3.7g Carbohydrates: 30.2g

Banana Chia Muffins

Total Time Taken: 1 hour
Yield: 12 Servings
Ingredients:

- ¼ cup whole milk
- ½ cup canola oil
- ½ cup white sugar
- ½ teaspoon salt
- 1 cup buttermilk
- 2 bananas, mashed
- 2 cups all-purpose flour
- 2 eggs
- 2 teaspoons baking powder
- 3 tablespoons chia seeds

Directions:

1. Mix the flour, chia seeds, sugar, salt and baking powder in a container.
2. Put in the remaining ingredients and stir for a few seconds to mix.
3. Spoon the batter in a muffin tin covered with muffin papers and preheat your oven and bake at 350F for about twenty minutes or until a toothpick inserted into the center of a muffin comes out clean.
4. Let them cool in the pan before you serve.

Nutritional Content of One Serving:

Calories: 266 Fat: 12.8g Protein: 5.7g Carbohydrates: 33.0g

Banana Chocolate Chip Muffins

Total Time Taken: 1 hour
Yield: 12 Servings
Ingredients:

- ¼ cup milk
- ½ cup dark chocolate chips
- ½ cup white sugar
- ½ teaspoon salt
- 1 ½ cups all-purpose flour
- 1 egg
- 1 teaspoon baking soda
- 1/3 cup butter, melted
- 3 bananas, mashed

Directions:

1. Mix the bananas, sugar, egg, butter and milk in a container until creamy.
2. Put in the remaining ingredients and fold them in using a spatula.
3. Spoon the batter into 12 muffin cups covered with muffin papers.
4. Pre-heat the oven and bake at 350F for about twenty minutes.

These muffins taste best chilled.

Nutritional Content of One Serving:

Calories: 191 Fat: 7.2g Protein: 2.9g Carbohydrates: 30.6g

Banana Crunch Muffins

Total Time Taken: 1 hour
Yield: 12 Servings
Ingredients:

- ¼ teaspoon salt
- ½ cup canola oil
- ½ cup light brown sugar
- ½ cup milk
- ½ cup shredded coconut
- 1 ½ teaspoons baking powder
- 1 cup rolled oats
- 1 teaspoon vanilla extract
- 2 bananas, mashed
- 2 cups all-purpose flour
- 2 eggs

Directions:

1. Mix the bananas, sugar, eggs, milk, vanilla and oil in a container.
2. Stir in the flour, salt, baking powder and coconut and mix using a spatula.

3. Spoon the batter in a muffin tin covered with muffin papers and top each muffin with rolled oats.
4. Pre-heat the oven and bake at 350F for about twenty minutes or until it rises significantly and starts to appear golden-brown.

These muffins taste best chilled.

Nutritional Content of One Serving:

Calories: 251 Fat: 11.8g Protein: 4.6g Carbohydrates: 32.3g

Banana Honey Muffins

Total Time Taken: 1 hour
Yield: 12 Servings
Ingredients:

- ½ cup buttermilk
- ½ cup honey
- ½ cup rolled oats
- ½ teaspoon salt
- 1 ½ cups all-purpose flour
- 1 egg
- 1 teaspoon baking soda
- 1 teaspoon vanilla extract
- 2 ripe bananas, mashed

Directions:

1. Mix the bananas, honey, buttermilk, egg and vanilla in a container.
2. Put in the remaining ingredients and mix using a spatula.
3. Spoon the batter in a muffin tin covered with muffin papers and preheat your oven and bake at 350F for about twenty minutes or until it rises significantly and starts to appear golden-brown.

These muffins taste best chilled.

Nutritional Content of One Serving:

Calories: 141 Fat: 0.9g Protein: 3.1g Carbohydrates: 30.9g

Cinnamon Oatmeal Cookies

Total Time Taken: 1 ¼ hours
Yield: 30 Servings
Ingredients:

- ¼ cup golden syrup
- 1 egg
- 2 cups rolled oats
- 1 teaspoon cinnamon powder
- ¼ teaspoon salt
- ½ teaspoon baking soda
- 2/3 cup butter
- 2/3 cup light brown sugar

- 2/3 cup all-purpose flour

Directions:

1. Mix the butter, sugar and syrup in a container until fluffy and creamy.
2. Put in the egg and mix thoroughly then fold in the remaining ingredients.
3. Drop spoonfuls of batter on a baking sheet coated with baking paper.
4. Preheat your oven and bake the cookies at 350F for about fifteen minutes or until a golden-brown colour is achieved on the edges.
5. Let the cookies cool down before you serve.

Nutritional Content of One Serving:

Calories: 89 Fat: 4.6g Protein: 1.2g Carbohydrates: 11.1g

Cinnamon Snap Cookies

Total Time Taken: 1 ¼ hours
Yield: 30 Servings

Ingredients:

- ¼ cup cocoa powder
- ½ teaspoon ground cloves
- ½ teaspoon ground ginger
- ½ teaspoon salt
- 1 cup butter, softened
- 1 egg
- 1 teaspoon baking soda
- 1 teaspoon cinnamon powder
- 1 teaspoon vanilla extract
- 2 cups all-purpose flour
- 2 tablespoons golden syrup
- 2/3 cup white sugar

Directions:

1. Mix the butter, sugar, vanilla and golden syrup in a container until pale and creamy.
2. Put in the egg and mix thoroughly then put in the flour mixture.
3. Make small balls of dough and place the cookies on a baking sheet coated with baking paper.
4. Preheat your oven and bake the cookies at 350F for about fifteen minutes until it is aromatic and appears golden brown.
5. These cookies taste best chilled.

Nutritional Content of One Serving:

Calories: 109 Fat: 6.5g Protein: 1.2g Carbohydrates: 12.3g

Cinnamon Sugar Cookies

Total Time Taken: 1 ½ hours
Yield: 25 Servings
Ingredients:

- ¼ teaspoon salt
- ½ cup coconut oil, melted
- ½ cup light brown sugar
- 1 cup white sugar
- 1 teaspoon baking powder
- 1 teaspoon cinnamon powder
- 1 teaspoon vanilla extract
- 2 cups all-purpose flour
- 2 eggs

Directions:

1. Mix the brown sugar and cinnamon in a container and set aside for later.
2. Combine the eggs and sugar in a separate container and stir until volume increases to twice what it was.
3. Put in the coconut oil and vanilla and mix thoroughly.
4. Put in the flour, salt and baking powder and mix using a spatula.
5. Make small balls of dough and roll them through cinnamon sugar.
6. Preheat your oven and bake the cookies at 350F for about fifteen minutes or until a golden-brown colour is achieved and fragrant.
7. These cookies taste best chilled.

Nutritional Content of One Serving:

Calories: 121 Fat: 4.8g Protein: 1.5g Carbohydrates: 18.6g

Clove Sugar Cookies

Total Time Taken: 1 ¼ hours
Yield: 30 Servings

Ingredients:

- ¼ teaspoon salt
- ½ cup powdered sugar
- ½ teaspoon baking powder
- 1 cup butter, softened
- 1 cup ground hazelnuts
- 1 egg yolk
- 1 teaspoon ground whole cloves
- 1 teaspoon vanilla extract
- 2 cups all-purpose flour

Directions:

1. Mix the butter and sugar in a container until pale and fluffy.
2. Put in the vanilla and egg yolk and mix thoroughly.
3. Fold in the flour, hazelnuts, cloves, salt and baking powder.
4. Transfer the dough to a floured working surface then roll the dough into a slim sheet.
5. Cut into small cookies with a cookie cutter and place them on a baking tray coated with baking paper.

6. Preheat your oven and bake the cookies at 350F for about fifteen minutes or until a golden-brown colour is achieved and fragrant.
7. These cookies taste best chilled.

Nutritional Content of One Serving:

Calories: 115 Fat: 7.9g Protein: 1.5g Carbohydrates: 9.7g

Coconut Butter Cookies

Total Time Taken: 1 ¼ hours
Yield: 20 Servings

Ingredients:

- ¼ teaspoon salt
- ½ cup coconut butter, softened
- 1 cup shredded coconut
- 1 egg
- 1 teaspoon baking powder
- 1 teaspoon coconut extract
- 2 cups all-purpose flour
- 2 tablespoons coconut oil
- 2/3 cup white sugar

Directions:

1. Mix the coconut butter, coconut oil and sugar in a container until pale and creamy.
2. Put in the egg and coconut extract and mix thoroughly.
3. Stir in the flour, coconut, baking powder and salt then form small balls of dough.
4. Put the balls on baking trays coated with baking paper and preheat your oven and bake at 350F for about fifteen minutes or until a golden-brown colour is achieved,
5. When finished, transfer the cookies in a container and dust them with powdered sugar.
6. These cookies taste best chilled.

Nutritional Content of One Serving:

Calories: 100 Fat: 3.0g Protein: 1.7g Carbohydrates: 17.0g

Coconut Florentine Cookies

Total Time Taken: 1 ¼ hours
Yield: 25 Servings

Ingredients:

- ¼ cup honey
- ¼ teaspoon salt
- ½ cup light brown sugar
- 1 ½ cups sliced almonds
- 1 cup butter, softened
- 1 cup shredded coconut
- 4 tablespoons all-purpose flour

Directions:

1. Mix the butter, sugar and honey in a heatproof container over a hot water bath until smooth and melted.
2. Turn off the heat and put in the coconut, almonds, salt and flour.
3. Drop spoonfuls of batter on a baking tray coated with baking paper.
4. Spread the mixture slightly then preheat your oven and bake the cookies at 350F for about fifteen minutes or until a golden-brown colour is achieved and crisp.
5. Let the cookies cool down before you serve.

Nutritional Content of One Serving:
Calories: 135 Fat: 11.3g Protein: 1.5g Carbohydrates: 8.3g

Coconut Lime Butter Cookies

Total Time Taken: 1 ¼ hours
Yield: 30 Servings

Ingredients:

- ½ teaspoon baking powder
- ½ teaspoon salt
- 1 cup butter, softened
- 1 cup shredded coconut
- 1 cup white sugar
- 1 lime, zested and juiced
- 1 teaspoon coconut extract
- 2 cups all-purpose flour
- 2 egg yolks

Directions:

1. Mix the butter and sugar in a container until creamy and pale.
2. Put in the egg yolks, lime zest and lime juice, as well as the coconut extract.
3. Stir in the flour, salt, coconut and baking powder then transfer the dough on a floured working surface.
4. Roll the dough into a slim sheet then cut small cookies using a cookie cutter of your choice.
5. Put the cookies on a baking tray covered with parchment paper.
6. Preheat your oven and bake the cookies at 350F for about fifteen minutes or until a golden-brown colour is achieved on the edges.
7. These cookies taste best chilled.

Nutritional Content of One Serving:
Calories: 124 Fat: 7.4g Protein: 1.2g Carbohydrates: 13.8g

Coconut Macaroons

Total Time Taken: 1 ½ hours
Yield: 20 Servings

Ingredients:

- ¼ teaspoon salt
- ½ cup all-purpose flour

- 1 can sweetened condensed milk
- 1 teaspoon vanilla extract
- 4 cups shredded coconut

Directions:

1. Mix the coconut, salt and flour in a container.
2. Put in the milk and vanilla and mix thoroughly.
3. Drop spoonfuls of mixture on baking trays coated with baking paper.
4. Preheat your oven and bake the cookies at 350F for fifteen minutes or until crisp and golden brown.
5. These cookies taste best chilled.

Nutritional Content of One Serving:

Calories: 118 Fat: 6.7g Protein: 2.1g Carbohydrates: 13.2g

Coconut Shortbread Cookies

Total Time Taken: 2 hours
Yield: 20 Servings
Ingredients:

- ¼ teaspoon baking powder
- ¼ teaspoon salt
- ½ cup powdered sugar
- 1 cup butter, softened
- 1 cup shredded coconut
- 1 egg
- 1 teaspoon coconut extract
- 2 cups all-purpose flour

Directions:

1. Mix the butter, sugar and coconut extract in a container.
2. Stir in the egg and mix thoroughly then put in the flour, salt, coconut and baking powder.
3. Wrap the dough in a plastic wrap and store in the refrigerator for about half an hour.
4. Transfer the dough to a working surface and roll it into a slim sheet.
5. Cut the dough into small cookies with a cookie cutter of your choice.
6. Put the cookies in a baking tray coated with baking paper.
7. Pre-heat the oven and bake at 350F for about fifteen minutes or until a golden-brown colour is achieved on the edges.
8. Best served chilled.

Nutritional Content of One Serving:

Calories: 157 Fat: 10.9g Protein: 1.8g Carbohydrates: 13.2g

Meringue Black Forest Cake

Total Time Taken: 2 ½ hours
Yield: 8 Servings
Ingredients:

- ¼ teaspoon salt
- ½ teaspoon cream of tartar
- 1 ½ cups dark chocolate chips
- 1 cup heavy cream
- 1 cup sour cherries, pitted
- 1 cup white sugar
- 1 teaspoon vanilla extract
- 2 tablespoons cocoa powder
- 4 egg whites

Directions:
1. Mix the egg whites, cream of tartar and salt in a container for minimum five minutes or until firm and fluffy.
2. Put in the sugar, progressively, whipping until shiny and firm.
3. Fold in the cocoa powder then spoon the meringue on a large baking sheet coated with baking paper, shaping it into two 8-inch rounds.
4. Pre-heat the oven and bake at 250F for about two hours.
5. Bring the cream to the boiling point in a saucepan. Put in the chocolate and stir until it melts completely. Allow this cream to cool down then put in the vanilla.
6. Layer the baked meringue with chocolate cream and sour cherries.
7. *Serve the cake fresh.*

Nutritional Content of One Serving:
Calories: 275 Fat: 11.8g Protein: 3.9g Carbohydrates: 44.1g

Milk Chocolate Chunk Cake

Total Time Taken: 1 1/5 hours
Yield: 12 Servings

Ingredients:
- ½ cup chocolate syrup
- ½ cup cocoa powder
- ½ teaspoon baking soda
- ½ teaspoon salt
- 1 cup butter, softened
- 1 cup buttermilk
- 1 cup white sugar
- 1 teaspoon baking powder
- 1 teaspoon vanilla extract
- 2 cups all-purpose flour
- 4 eggs
- 8 oz. milk chocolate, chopped

Directions:
1. Sift the flour, cocoa powder, baking powder, baking soda and salt.

2. Mix the butter with sugar until creamy and fluffy. Put in the chocolate syrup then mix in the eggs and vanilla.

3. Fold in the flour, alternating it with buttermilk. Begin and finish with flour.

4. Put in the chocolate chunks then spoon the batter in a round cake pan coated with baking paper.

5. Pre-heat the oven and bake at 350F for about forty minutes or until a toothpick comes out clean after being inserted into the center of the cake.

Nutritional Content of One Serving:

Calories: 449 Fat: 23.4g Protein: 7.2g Carbohydrates: 55.2g

Mississippi Mud Cake

Total Time Taken: 1 ¼ hours
Yield: 12 Servings

Ingredients:

- ½ cup cocoa powder
- ½ teaspoon salt
- 1 cup buttermilk
- 1 cup canola oil
- 1 cup hot coffee
- 1 teaspoon baking powder
- 1 teaspoon baking soda
- 2 ½ cups all-purpose flour
- 2 cups white sugar
- 2 eggs
- 2 teaspoons vanilla extract

Directions:

1. Mix the sugar, eggs, coffee, oil, vanilla and buttermilk in a container.

2. In a separate container, mix the cocoa powder, salt, flour, baking soda and baking powder then mix in the coffee mixture.

3. Pour the batter in a 10-inch round cake pan covered with parchment paper.

4. Pre-heat the oven and bake at 330F for about fifty minutes.

5. Let the cake cool in the pan and serve, sliced.

Nutritional Content of One Serving:

Calories: 410 Fat: 19.8g Protein: 5.0g Carbohydrates: 56.5g

Moist Apple Cake

Total Time Taken: 1 ½ hours
Yield: 14 Servings

Ingredients:

- ¼ cup maple syrup
- ½ teaspoon salt
- 1 ½ cups light brown sugar

- 1 cup butter, softened
- 1 teaspoon cinnamon powder
- 1 teaspoon ground cardamom
- 1 teaspoon ground ginger
- 2 cups applesauce
- 2 eggs
- 2 green apples, peeled, cored and diced
- 2 teaspoons baking soda
- 3 cups all-purpose flour

Directions:

1. Mix the flour, baking soda, salt and spices in a container.
2. In a separate container, mix the butter, sugar and maple syrup and stir thoroughly for a few minutes.
3. Stir in the eggs and applesauce then fold in the flour mixture.
4. Put in the apples then spoon the batter in a 10-inch round cake pan coated with baking paper.
5. Pre-heat the oven and bake at 350F for about fifty minutes or until a toothpick inserted into the center of the cake comes out clean.
6. Let the cake cool in the pan and serve, sliced.

Nutritional Content of One Serving:

Calories: 326 Fat: 14.1g Protein: 3.9g Carbohydrates: 47.2g

Moist Chocolate Cake

Total Time Taken: 1 ¼ hours
Yield: 12 Servings

Ingredients:

- ½ cup canola oil
- ½ cup cocoa powder
- ½ teaspoon salt
- 1 ½ teaspoon baking powder
- 1 cup buttermilk
- 1 cup hot coffee
- 1 teaspoon vanilla extract
- 2 cups all-purpose flour
- 2 cups white sugar
- 2 eggs

Directions:

1. Mix the sugar, eggs and canola oil in a container until creamy.
2. Stir in the vanilla, coffee and buttermilk then put in the remaining ingredients.
3. Pour the batter in a 9-inch round cake pan coated with baking paper.
4. Pre-heat the oven and bake at 350F for about forty-five minutes or until a toothpick comes out clean after being inserted into the center of the cake.
5. Let the cake cool in the pan before you serve.

Nutritional Content of One Serving:
Calories: 310 Fat: 10.7g Protein: 4.4g Carbohydrates: 52.6g

Moist Pumpkin Cake

Total Time Taken: 1 ¼ hours
Yield: 12 Servings

Ingredients:

- ¼ teaspoon ground nutmeg
- ½ teaspoon ground ginger
- ½ teaspoon salt
- 1 ½ cups pumpkin puree
- 1 cup canola oil
- 1 teaspoon cinnamon powder
- 2 cups white sugar
- 2 teaspoons baking powder
- 3 cups all-purpose flour
- 4 eggs

Directions:

1. Mix the sugar, canola oil and eggs in a container until creamy and volume increases to twice what it was.
2. Stir in the pumpkin puree, then fold in the remaining ingredients.
3. Pour the batter in a 9-inch round cake pan coated with baking paper.
4. Pre-heat the oven and bake at 350F for around forty minutes or until well risen and fragrant.
5. Let the cake cool in the pan and serve, sliced.

Nutritional Content of One Serving:
Calories: 432 Fat: 20.1g Protein: 5.4g Carbohydrates: 60.2g

Molasses Pear Bundt Cake

Total Time Taken: 1 ¼ hours
Yield: 10 Servings

Ingredients:

- ½ cup light brown sugar
- ½ cup molasses
- ½ cup sour cream
- ½ cup whole milk
- ½ teaspoon ground ginger
- ½ teaspoon salt
- 1 cup butter, softened
- 1 teaspoon all-spice
- 1 teaspoon baking powder
- 1 teaspoon baking soda

- 1 teaspoon cinnamon powder
- 2 cups all-purpose flour
- 2 pears, peeled, cored and diced
- 3 eggs

Directions:
1. Mix the butter, molasses and sugar in a container until creamy and pale.
2. Stir in the eggs, one at a time, stirring thoroughly after each addition.
3. Mix the flour with baking powder, baking soda, salt and spices.
4. Mix the milk with cream.
5. Fold the flour into the butter mixture, alternating it with the milk and sour cream mix.
6. Put in the pears then spoon the batter in a greased Bundt cake pan.
7. Pre-heat the oven and bake at 350F for about forty minutes or until a toothpick inserted in the center comes out clean.
8. Let the cake cool in the pan for about ten minutes then flip over on a platter.
9. Serve chilled.

Nutritional Content of One Serving:
Calories: 405 Fat: 22.9g Protein: 5.3g Carbohydrates: 46.3g

Morello Cherry Cake

Total Time Taken: 1 ¼ hours
Yield: 12 Servings

Ingredients:
- ¼ cup brandy
- ½ cup cocoa powder
- ½ cup cocoa powder
- ½ cup coconut oil, melted
- ½ cup white sugar
- ½ teaspoon salt
- ¾ cup all-purpose flour
- 1 cup almond flour
- 1 cup maple syrup
- 1 cup Morello cherries
- 3 eggs

Directions:
1. Mix the maple syrup, coconut oil, brandy and eggs in a container.
2. Stir in the sugar and mix thoroughly.
3. Fold in the cocoa powder, almond flour, all-purpose flour, salt and cocoa powder.
4. Spoon the batter in a 9-inch round cake pan and top with cherries.
5. Pre-heat the oven and bake at 350F for forty minutes.
6. *The cake tastes best chilled.*

Nutritional Content of One Serving:

Calories: 270 Fat: 12.4g Protein: 4.2g Carbohydrates: 40.9g

Natural Red Velvet Cake

Total Time Taken: 1 ¼ hours
Yield: 10 Servings
Ingredients:
Cake:

- ¼ cup white sugar
- ½ cup canola oil
- ½ cup light brown sugar
- ½ teaspoon cinnamon powder
- ½ teaspoon salt
- 1 ¼ cups all-purpose flour
- 1 teaspoon baking powder
- 2 beetroots, peeled and pureed
- 2 eggs
- 2 tablespoons cornstarch

Frosting:

- ¼ cup butter, softened
- 1 cup cream cheese
- 1 cup powdered sugar

Directions:

1. For the cake, combine the beetroot puree, canola oil, eggs and sugar in a container.
2. Stir in the remaining ingredients and mix thoroughly.
3. Pour the batter in a 8-inch round cake pan coated with baking paper.
4. Pre-heat the oven and bake at 350F for forty minutes.
5. When finished, allow the cake to cool in the pan then transfer the cake on a platter.
6. For the frosting, combine all the ingredients in a container until fluffy.
7. Cover the cake with the frosting and serve it fresh.

Nutritional Content of One Serving:
Calories: 395 Fat: 24.7g Protein: 4.8g Carbohydrates: 40.1g

Olive Oil Pistachio Cake

Total Time Taken: 1 hour
Yield: 10 Servings
Ingredients:

- ½ cup corn meal
- ½ cup extra virgin olive oil
- ½ cup ground pistachios
- ½ cup white sugar
- 3 eggs

- ½ cup whole milk
- ½ teaspoon salt
- 1 cup all-purpose flour
- 1 teaspoon baking powder
- 1 teaspoon baking soda
- 2 tablespoons orange zest

Directions:

1. Mix the dry ingredients in a container.
2. In a separate container, mix the oil, sugar, eggs and orange zest and stir thoroughly for a few minutes until volume increases to twice what it was.
3. Stir in the milk, followed by the dry ingredients.
4. Pour the batter in 10-inch round cake pan coated with baking paper.
5. Preheat your oven and bake the cake for around forty minutes.
6. The cake tastes best chilled.

Nutritional Content of One Serving:

Calories: 221 Fat: 12.1g Protein: 4.0g Carbohydrates: 26.1g

Orange Chocolate Cake

Total Time Taken: 1 ¼ hours
Yield: 12 Servings

Ingredients:

- ½ cup candied orange peel, chopped
- ½ teaspoon salt
- 1 cup white sugar
- 1 teaspoon baking soda
- 2 cups ground almonds
- 4 eggs
- 8 oz. dark chocolate, melted

Directions:

1. Mix the eggs with sugar until fluffy and pale.
2. Stir in the melted chocolate then put in the almonds, baking soda and salt.
3. Fold in the candied orange peel then pour the batter in 1 8-inch round cake pan coated with baking paper.
4. Pre-heat the oven and bake at 350F for about half an hour.
5. Let the cake cool in the pan before you serve.

Nutritional Content of One Serving:

Calories: 280 Fat: 15.0g Protein: 6.7g Carbohydrates: 32.4g

Orange Chocolate Mud Cake

Total Time Taken: 1 ¼ hours
Yield: 10 Servings

Ingredients:

- ½ cup brewed coffee
- ½ cup candied orange peel, chopped
- ½ teaspoon salt
- ¾ cup cocoa powder
- 1 ½ cups all-purpose flour
- 1 cup butter, softened
- 1 tablespoon orange zest
- 1 teaspoon baking soda
- 1 teaspoon vanilla extract
- 2 cups white sugar
- 2 tablespoons cornstarch
- 4 eggs

Directions:

1. Mix the sugar and butter in a container until fluffy and pale.
2. Put in the coffee, eggs, vanilla and orange zest.
3. Stir in the remaining ingredients and mix thoroughly.
4. Pour the batter in a 9-inch round cake pan coated with baking paper.
5. Preheat your oven and bake the cake for about fifty minutes or until the cake looks set.
6. *The cake tastes best chilled.*

Nutritional Content of One Serving:

Calories: 433 Fat: 21.2g Protein: 5.6g Carbohydrates: 60.9g

Orange Pound Cake

Total Time Taken: 1 ¼ hours
 Yield: 16 Servings

Ingredients:

- ½ teaspoon salt
- 1 ½ cups butter, softened
- 1 cup sour cream
- 1 orange, zested and juiced
- 1 teaspoon vanilla extract
- 2 cups white sugar
- 2 teaspoons baking powder
- 3 cups all-purpose flour
- 6 eggs

Directions:

1. Sift the flour with salt and baking powder.
2. Mix the butter with sugar for five minutes until creamy and fluffy.
3. Put in the vanilla, orange zest and orange juice and mix thoroughly.

4. Stir in the sour cream then fold in the flour mixture.
5. Pour the batter in a large loaf cake pan coated with baking paper.
6. Pre-heat the oven and bake at 330F for forty minutes then turn the heat on 350F for another ten minutes.
7. Let the cake cool in the pan and serve, sliced.

Nutritional Content of One Serving:
Calories: 393 Fat: 22.2g Protein: 5.2g Carbohydrates: 45.3g

Orange Pumpkin Bundt Cake

Total Time Taken: 1 ¼ hours
Yield: 12 Servings

Ingredients:
- ½ teaspoon cinnamon powder
- ½ teaspoon ground cardamom
- ½ teaspoon ground ginger
- ½ teaspoon salt
- ¾ cup butter, softened
- 1 ¼ cups white sugar
- 1 ½ teaspoons baking soda
- 1 cup pumpkin puree
- 1 orange, zested and juiced
- 1 teaspoon vanilla extract
- 2 ½ cups all-purpose flour
- 4 eggs

Directions:
1. Mix the butter with sugar in a container until creamy and fluffy.
2. Stir in the eggs and vanilla and mix thoroughly then put in the orange zest and juice, as well as pumpkin puree.
3. Fold in the rest of the ingredients then spoon the batter in a loaf cake pan coated with baking paper.
4. Preheat your oven and bake the cake for about forty minutes.
5. Let the cake cool in the pan before you serve.

Nutritional Content of One Serving:
Calories: 311 Fat: 13.3g Protein: 5.0g Carbohydrates: 44.4g

Orange Ricotta Cake

Total Time Taken: 1 ¼ hours
Yield: 10 Servings

Ingredients:
- ½ cup all-purpose flour
- ½ cup white chocolate, chopped
- ¾ cup white sugar

- 1 cup fresh raspberries
- 1 teaspoon baking powder
- 1 teaspoon orange zest
- 1 teaspoon vanilla extract
- 3 cups ricotta cheese
- 3 eggs

Directions:

1. Mix the ricotta cheese, vanilla, orange zest, sugar and eggs in a container.
2. Stir in rest of the ingredients then spoon the batter in a 9-inch round cake pan coated with baking paper.
3. Pre-heat the oven and bake at 350F for around forty minutes or until a golden-brown colour is achieved.
4. The cake tastes best chilled.

Nutritional Content of One Serving:

Calories: 255 Fat: 10.1g Protein: 11.4g Carbohydrates: 30.5g

Parsnip Carrot Cake

Total Time Taken: 1 ½ hours
Yield: 12 Servings

Ingredients:

- ¼ cup white sugar
- ½ cup walnuts, chopped
- ½ teaspoon salt
- 1 cup canola oil
- 1 cup crushed pineapple
- 1 cup grated carrots
- 1 cup grated parsnips
- 1 cup light brown sugar
- 1 teaspoon baking powder
- 1 teaspoon baking soda
- 1 teaspoon cinnamon powder
- 1 teaspoon ground ginger
- 2 cups all-purpose flour
- 4 eggs

Directions:

1. Mix the flour, salt, baking soda, baking powder and spices in a container.
2. In a separate container, combine the eggs with the sugars until fluffy and pale.
3. Put in the oil then mix in the carrots, parsnips, pineapple and walnuts.
4. Fold in the dry ingredients you readied a while back.
5. Pour the batter in a 9-inch round cake pan coated with baking paper.
6. Pre-heat the oven and bake at 350F for about forty minutes or until a toothpick inserted in the center comes out clean.
7. Sprinkle with powdered sugar and serve chilled.

Nutritional Content of One Serving:
Calories: 371 Fat: 23.0g Protein: 5.5g Carbohydrates: 37.6g

Peach Brandy Cake

Total Time Taken: 1 ½ hours
Yield: 10 Servings
Ingredients:

Cake:

- ½ cup butter, melted
- ½ teaspoon salt
- 1 cup sweet red win
- 1 cup white sugar
- 1 teaspoon baking powder
- 1 teaspoon ground cardamom
- 2 cups almond flour
- 4 peaches, pitted and sliced Brandy
- 5 eggs

Glaze:

- 1 cup powdered sugar
- 1 tablespoon brandy

Directions:

1. To prepare the cake, combine the almond flour, baking powder, salt and cinnamon.
2. In a separate container, combine the sugar and eggs until fluffy and pale. Put in the butter and mix thoroughly, then mix in the red wine.
3. Fold in the almond flour then pour the batter in a 9-inch round cake pan coated with baking paper.
4. Top with sliced peaches and preheat your oven and bake at 350F for 45 minutes or until a toothpick comes out clean after being inserted into the center of the cake.
5. Let the cake cool in the pan then move it to a platter.
6. For the glaze, combine the sugar with brandy. Sprinkle the glaze over the cake and serve it fresh.

Nutritional Content of One Serving:
Calories: 317 Fat: 15.8g Protein: 8.3g Carbohydrates: 37.4g

Peach Meringue Cake

Total Time Taken: 1 ½ hours
Yield: 10 Servings
Ingredients:

Cake:

- ½ cup butter, softened
- ½ cup canola oil
- ½ cup plain yogurt
- ½ teaspoon salt

- ¾ cup white sugar
- 1 teaspoon baking soda
- 1 teaspoon vanilla extract
- 2 cups all-purpose flour
- 3 eggs
- 3 peaches, pitted and sliced

Meringue:
- ½ cup white sugar
- 1 teaspoon vanilla extract
- 3 egg whites

Directions:
1. For the cake, combine the butter, oil and sugar in a container until fluffy and creamy.
2. Stir in the egg, vanilla and yogurt and mix thoroughly.
3. Fold in the flour, baking soda and salt then spoon the batter in a round cake pan coated with baking paper.
4. Top with peach slices and preheat your oven and bake at 350F for about forty minutes or until it rises significantly and starts to appear golden-brown.
5. While the cake bakes, combine the egg whites and sugar in a heatproof container.
6. Place over a hot water bath and mix with a whisk until the mixture is hot.
7. Turn off the heat and continue mixing until firm and shiny. Put in the vanilla and mix thoroughly.
8. Spoon the meringue over the hot cake and allow to cool.
9. *Serve immediately.*

Nutritional Content of One Serving:
Calories: 411 Fat: 21.9g Protein: 6.4g Carbohydrates: 48.5g

Peach Upside Down Cake

Total Time Taken: 1 hour
Yield: 8 Servings
Ingredients:
- ¼ cup butter, melted
- ¼ cup whole milk
- ¼ teaspoon salt
- 1 egg
- ½ cup light brown sugar
- ½ cup sour cream
- 1 cup all-purpose flour
- 1 teaspoon baking powder
- 2 tablespoons butter
- 4 peaches, sliced

Directions:
1. Position the peaches at the bottom of a 9-inch round cake pan coated with baking paper.

2. Drizzle with brown sugar and top with a few pieces of butter.
3. For the batter, combine the flour, baking powder and salt in a container. Put in the rest of the ingredients and stir for a few seconds to mix.
4. Spoon the batter over the peaches and preheat your oven and bake at 350F for about half an hour.
5. When finished, flip the cake upside down on a platter.
6. Serve chilled.

Nutritional Content of One Serving:
Calories: 231 Fat: 12.7g Protein: 3.6g Carbohydrates: 26.8g

Peanut Butter Chocolate Bundt Cake

Total Time Taken: 1 ¼ hours
Yield: 10 Servings

Ingredients:

- ¼ cup butter, softened
- ½ cup cocoa powder
- ½ cup dark chocolate chips
- ½ teaspoon baking soda
- ½ teaspoon salt
- 1 cup buttermilk
- 1 cup light brown sugar
- 1 cup smooth peanut butter
- 1 teaspoon vanilla extract
- 2 cups all-purpose flour
- 2 teaspoons baking powder
- 3 eggs

Directions:

1. Sift the flour, baking powder, baking soda, salt and cocoa powder.
2. Mix the peanut butter, butter and sugar in a container until creamy and light.
3. Put in the eggs and mix thoroughly then mix in the vanilla.
4. Fold in the flour, alternating it with buttermilk. Begin and finish with flour.
5. Put in the chocolate chips then spoon the batter in a Bundt cake pan lined using butter.
6. Preheat your oven and bake the cake for about forty minutes or until it rises significantly and starts to appear golden-brown.
7. When finished, flip the cake upside down on a platter and serve chilled.

Nutritional Content of One Serving:
Calories: 407 Fat: 21.6g Protein: 12.8g Carbohydrates: 46.5g

Peanut Butter Jelly Cake

Total Time Taken: 1 ½ hours
Yield: 12 Servings

Ingredients:

- ½ cup butter, softened
- ½ cup cranberry jelly
- ½ cup light brown sugar
- ½ cup peanut butter
- ½ cup whole milk
- ½ teaspoon salt
- 1 cup white sugar
- 1 teaspoon vanilla extract
- 2 cups all-purpose flour
- 2 eggs
- 2 tablespoons canola oil
- 2 teaspoons baking powder

Directions:

1. Sift the flour, baking powder and salt.
2. Mix the peanut butter, butter, canola oil and sugars in a container until creamy and fluffy.
3. Stir in the eggs and vanilla and mix thoroughly.
4. Fold in the flour mixture, alternating it with the milk. Begin and finish with flour.
5. Spoon the batter in a round cake pan coated with baking paper.
6. Pre-heat the oven and bake at 350F for about forty minutes or until a toothpick inserted into the center of the cake comes out clean.
7. When finished, brush the cake with cranberry jelly and serve it fresh.

Nutritional Content of One Serving:

Calories: 334 Fat: 16.7g Protein: 6.2g Carbohydrates: 42.0g

Pear Brownie Cake

Total Time Taken: 1 ¼ hours
Yield: 10 Servings

Ingredients:

- ¼ cup cocoa powder
- ¼ teaspoon salt
- ½ cup all-purpose flour
- ½ cup butter, softened
- ½ cup white sugar
- 1 cup dark chocolate chips
- 2 pears, peeled, cored and diced
- 4 eggs

Directions:

1. Mix the butter and chocolate in a heatproof container over a hot water bath. Melt them together until the desired smoothness is achieved.
2. Put in the eggs, one at a time, then mix in the sugar.

3. Fold in the flour, cocoa powder and salt then spoon the batter in a 8-inch round cake pan coated with baking paper.
4. Top with pear dices and preheat your oven and bake at 350F for 25 minutes.
5. Let the cake cool in the pan before you serve.

Nutritional Content of One Serving:
Calories: 252 Fat: 14.6g Protein: 4.3g Carbohydrates: 30.5g

Pear Cinnamon Bundt Cake

Total Time Taken: 1 ¼ hours
Yield: 10 Servings

Ingredients:
- ½ cup buttermilk
- ½ teaspoon ground ginger
- ½ teaspoon salt
- 1 ½ cups light brown sugar
- 1 cup butter, melted
- 1 teaspoon cinnamon powder
- 2 cups all-purpose flour
- 2 pears, peeled, cored and diced
- 2 teaspoons baking powder
- 4 eggs

Directions:
1. Mix the flour, cinnamon, ginger, baking powder and salt in a container.
2. In a separate container, mix the butter, sugar, eggs and buttermilk and mix thoroughly. Pour this mixture over the dry ingredients then fold in the pears.
3. Spoon the batter in a Bundt cake pan lined using butter.
4. Pre-heat the oven and bake at 350F for around forty minutes or until golden and it rises significantly.
5. Let the cake cool in the pan before you serve.

Nutritional Content of One Serving:
Calories: 392 Fat: 20.6g Protein: 5.6g Carbohydrates: 48.0g

Pecan Butter Cake

Total Time Taken: 1 ¼ hours
Yield: 12 Servings

Ingredients:
- ½ cup butter, softened
- ½ teaspoon salt
- 1 ½ cups pecans, chopped
- 1 ½ teaspoons baking powder
- 1 cup pecan butter
- 1 cup white sugar

- 1 teaspoon lemon zest
- 1 teaspoon vanilla extract
- 2 cups all-purpose flour
- 4 eggs

Directions:

1. Mix the two types of butter with sugar until creamy and light.
2. Stir in the eggs, one at a time, then put in the vanilla and lemon zest then fold in the dry ingredients.
3. Spoon the batter in a 9-inch round cake pan coated with baking paper.
4. Pre-heat the oven and bake at 350F for about forty minutes or until it rises significantly and starts to appear golden-brown.
5. Let the cake cool in the pan then sprinkle it with powdered sugar and serve.

Nutritional Content of One Serving:

Calories: 377 Fat: 24.2g Protein: 6.2g Carbohydrates: 37.9g

Pecan Carrot Bundt Cake

Total Time Taken: 1 ½ hours
Yield: 14 Servings

Ingredients:

- ¼ cup orange juice
- ½ cup dark brown sugar
- ½ teaspoon baking powder
- ½ teaspoon cardamom powder
- ½ teaspoon salt
- 1 cup butter, softened
- 1 cup crushed pineapple
- 1 cup white sugar
- 1 tablespoon lemon zest
- 1 tablespoon orange zest
- 1 teaspoon baking soda
- 1 teaspoon cinnamon powder
- 2 ½ cups all-purpose flour
- 2 cups grated carrots
- 4 eggs

Directions:

1. Sift the flour, baking soda, baking powder, salt and spices in a container.
2. In a separate container, combine the butter and sugars until creamy and fluffy.
3. Stir in the eggs, one at a time, then put in the citrus zest, carrots, orange juice and pineapple.
4. Fold in the flour and stir lightly using a spatula.
5. Pour the batter in a greased Bundt cake pan.
6. Pre-heat the oven and bake at 350F for about fifty minutes or until a toothpick inserted into the center of the cake comes out clean.

7. Let the cake cool in the pan before you serve.

Nutritional Content of One Serving:

Calories: 304 Fat: 14.6g Protein: 4.3g Carbohydrates: 40.4g

Pecan Rum Cake

Total Time Taken: 1 ¼ hours
Yield: 12 Servings
Ingredients:

Cake:

- ¼ cup dark rum
- ½ cup whole milk
- ½ teaspoon salt
- 1 ¼ cups all-purpose flour
- 1 cup butter, softened
- 1 cup ground pecans
- 1 cup white sugar
- 1 teaspoon baking soda
- 1 teaspoon vanilla extract
- 3 eggs

Glaze:

- 1 cup powdered sugar
- 1 tablespoon dark rum

Directions:

1. For the cake, combine the flour with baking soda, salt and pecans.
2. In a separate container, combine the butter and sugar until fluffy and creamy.
3. Stir in the eggs, one after another, then put in the vanilla, rum and milk and mix thoroughly.
4. Fold in the pecan and flour mixture then spoon the batter in a 8-inch round cake pan coated with baking paper.
5. Pre-heat the oven and bake at 350F for around forty minutes or until well risen and fragrant.
6. Let the cake cool in the pan then move to a platter.
7. For the glaze, combine the ingredients in a container. Sprinkle the glaze over the cake and serve fresh.

Nutritional Content of One Serving:

Calories: 329 Fat: 17.8g Protein: 3.3g Carbohydrates: 37.3g

Peppermint Chocolate Cake

Total Time Taken: 1 ¼ hours
Yield: 10 Servings
Ingredients:

Cake:

- ½ cup canola oil
- 1 cup buttermilk

- ½ cup cocoa powder
- ½ cup hot coffee
- ½ teaspoon baking soda
- ½ teaspoon salt
- 1 ½ cups all-purpose flour
- 1 teaspoon baking powder
- 1 teaspoon vanilla extract

Frosting:
- ½ cup butter, softened
- 1 ½ cups powdered sugar
- 1 teaspoon peppermint extract
- 3 oz. dark chocolate, melted and cooled

Directions:
1. To prepare the cake, combine the dry ingredients in a container and the wet ingredients in a separate container.
2. Combine the flour mixture with the wet ingredients and stir for a few seconds to mix.
3. Pour the batter in a 9-inch cake pan coated with baking paper.
4. Pre-heat the oven and bake at 350F for about 35 minutes.
5. Let the cake cool in the pan then move to a platter.
6. For the frosting, combine the butter with the sugar until creamy and fluffy.
7. Put in the peppermint extract and the melted chocolate and mix thoroughly.
8. Frost the top of the cake with this chocolate buttercream and serve immediately or place in your refrigerator.

Nutritional Content of One Serving:
Calories: 384 Fat: 23.6g Protein: 4.3g Carbohydrates: 41.2g

Pistachio Bundt Cake

Total Time Taken: 1 hour
Yield: 10 Servings
Ingredients:
- ½ teaspoon salt
- ¾ cup butter, softened
- 1 ½ cups all-purpose flour
- 1 ½ teaspoons baking powder
- 1 cup ground pistachio
- 1 cup white sugar
- 1 teaspoon vanilla extract
- 4 eggs

Directions:
1. Mix the butter and sugar until pale and light. Stir in the eggs and vanilla and mix thoroughly.
2. Fold in the flour, pistachio, baking powder and salt then spoon the batter in a greased Bundt cake pan.

3. Pre-heat the oven and bake at 350F for about forty minutes or until it rises significantly and starts to appear golden- brown.
4. Let the cake cool in the pan before you serve.

Nutritional Content of One Serving:
Calories: 292 Fat: 15.7g Protein: 4.3g Carbohydrates: 34.9g

Pistachio Cake

Total Time Taken: 1 hour
Yield: 8 Servings
Ingredients:
- ¼ cup whole milk
- ¼ teaspoon cinnamon powder
- ¼ teaspoon salt
- ½ cup all-purpose flour
- ½ cup butter, softened
- ½ cup white sugar
- ½ teaspoon ground cardamom
- 1 cup ground pistachio
- 1 teaspoon baking powder
- 1 teaspoon lemon zest
- 2 eggs

Directions:
1. Mix the pistachio, flour, salt, baking powder, cardamom and cinnamon in a container.
2. Mix the butter and sugar in a container until fluffy and light. Stir in the eggs and milk, as well as lemon zest.
3. Fold in the flour and pistachio mixture then spoon the batter in a 8-inch round cake pan coated with baking paper.
4. Pre-heat the oven and bake at 350F for around forty minutes.
5. The cake tastes best chilled, dusted with powdered sugar.

Nutritional Content of One Serving:
Calories: 214 Fat: 14.1g Protein: 3.2g Carbohydrates: 20.1g

Plum Polenta Cake

Total Time Taken: 1 hour
Yield: 8 Servings
Ingredients:
- ½ cup butter, softened
- ½ cup honey
- ½ pound plums, pitted and sliced
- ½ teaspoon salt
- ½ teaspoon salt
- 1 cup instant polenta flour

- 1 tablespoon lemon zest
- 1 teaspoon baking soda
- 2 cups whole milk
- 4 eggs

Directions:

1. Mix the butter with honey until creamy and firm. Stir in the eggs, one at a time, then put in the milk and lemon zest.
2. Fold in the polenta flour, baking soda and salt then pour the batter in a 9-inch round cake pan coated with baking paper.
3. Top with plum slices and preheat your oven and bake at 350F for around forty minutes or until a golden-brown colour is achieved and it rises significantly.
4. Let the cake cool in the pan then serve, sliced.

Nutritional Content of One Serving:

Calories: 298 Fat: 15.7g Protein: 7.1g Carbohydrates: 33.7g

Pomegranate Cake

Total Time Taken: 1 ½ hours
Yield: 10 Servings
Ingredients:

White cake:

- ½ teaspoon salt
- ¾ cup whole milk
- 1 ¼ cups butter, softened
- 1 ½ cups all-purpose flour
- 1 ½ teaspoons baking powder
- 1 cup white sugar
- 1 teaspoon lemon zest
- 1 teaspoon vanilla extract
- 4 eggs whites

Pomegranate frosting:

- ¼ cup pomegranate juice
- 1 cup white sugar 1 pinch salt
- 4 egg whites

Directions:

1. Mix the flour with sugar, baking powder, salt and butter in a container until grainy.
2. Combine the egg whites with milk, vanilla and lemon zest in a container then pour this mixture over the flour mixture.
3. Stir slowly until mixed then spoon the batter into two 7-inch circular cake pans coated with baking paper.
4. Pre-heat the oven and bake at 350F for about half an hour.
5. Let the cakes cool in the pan then level them and cut each cake in half along the length.

6. For the frosting, combine all the ingredients in a heatproof container and place over a hot water bath. Keep over heat, stirring constantly, until the mixture is hot.
7. Turn off the heat and whip using an electric mixer for minimum seven minutes until firm and shiny.
8. Use half of the frosting to fill the cake and the rest of the frosting to frost the cake.
9. Serve immediately or place in your refrigerator.

Nutritional Content of One Serving:
Calories: 449 Fat: 23.8g Protein: 5.7g Carbohydrates: 55.8g

Poppy Seed Lemon Bundt Cake

Total Time Taken: 1 ¼ hours
Yield: 12 Servings

Ingredients:
- ½ cup cornstarch
- ½ cup sour cream
- ½ teaspoon salt
- 1 cup butter, softened
- 1 cup white sugar
- 1 tablespoon lemon zest
- 1 teaspoon baking powder
- 1 teaspoon baking soda
- 1 teaspoon vanilla extract
- 2 cups all-purpose flour
- 2 tablespoons lemon juice
- 2 tablespoons poppy seeds
- 4 eggs

Directions:
1. Sift the flour, cornstarch, baking powder, baking soda and salt then mix it with the poppy seeds.
2. Mix the butter and sugar in a container until creamy and fluffy.
3. Stir in the eggs, lemon zest and lemon juice and mix thoroughly.
4. Fold in the flour mixture then put in the sour cream and mix thoroughly.
5. Spoon the batter in a greased Bundt cake pan and preheat your oven and bake at 350F for about forty minutes or until a toothpick comes out clean after being inserted into the center of the cake.
6. Let the cake cool in the pan before you serve.

Nutritional Content of One Serving:
Calories: 346 Fat: 19.7g Protein: 4.8g Carbohydrates: 38.7g

Rainbow Cake

Total Time Taken: 1 hour
Yield: 10 Servings
Ingredients:
- ½ cup sour cream

- ½ teaspoon baking soda
- ½ teaspoon salt
- 1 ½ cups white sugar
- 1 cup butter, softened
- 1 teaspoon baking powder
- 1 teaspoon vanilla extract
- 2 ½ cups all-purpose flour
- 2 whole eggs
- 3 egg whites
- Red, green, blue and yellow food coloring

Directions:

1. Mix the butter and sugar in a container until fluffy and creamy.
2. Stir in the eggs, egg whites, vanilla and sour cream and stir thoroughly for a few minutes.
3. Mix the flour with baking powder, baking soda and salt then fold it in the batter.
4. Divide the batter into 4 smaller containers then add a drop of food colouring into each container and stir gently using a spoon in each batch of batter.
5. Spoon the colourful batter into a 9-inch cake pan coated with baking paper.
6. Use a toothpick to swirl the batter around until colours are blended.
7. Pre-heat the oven and bake at 350F for around forty minutes.
8. Let the cake cool in the pan then serve, sliced.

Nutritional Content of One Serving:

Calories: 433 Fat: 22.0g Protein: 6.0g Carbohydrates: 54.8g

Raspberry Chocolate Cake

Total Time Taken: 1 ¼ hours
Yield: 10 Servings

Ingredients:

- ½ cup butter, melted
- ½ teaspoon baking powder
- ½ teaspoon salt
- 1 ¼ cups all-purpose flour
- 1 cup white sugar
- 1 teaspoon vanilla extract
- 2 cups fresh raspberries
- 3 oz. dark chocolate, melted
- 6 eggs

Directions:

1. Mix the eggs and sugar in a container until its volume increases to almost three times it was.
2. Stir in the melted butter and chocolate, as well as vanilla.
3. Fold in the baking powder and salt then put in the raspberries and stir lightly.

4. Pour the batter in a 9-inch round cake pan and preheat your oven and bake at 350F for around forty minutes or until a toothpick inserted into the center of the cake comes out clean.

5. Let cool in the pan then serve, sliced.

Nutritional Content of One Serving:

Calories: 311 Fat: 14.7g Protein: 6.0g Carbohydrates: 40.3g

Raspberry Chocolate Mud Cake

Total Time Taken: 1 ½ hours
Yield: 12 Servings

Ingredients:

- ½ cup buttermilk
- ½ cup cocoa powder
- ½ cup heavy cream
- ½ teaspoon salt
- 1 ½ cups fresh raspberries
- 1 ½ cups white sugar
- 1 cup butter, softened
- 1 cup dark chocolate chips
- 1 cup hot water
- 2 cups all-purpose flour
- 2 tablespoons brandy
- 2 teaspoons baking powder
- 3 eggs

Directions:

1. Mix the butter and chocolate chips in a heatproof container and place over a hot water bath. Melt them together until the desired smoothness is achieved.
2. Stir in the sugar and hot water and mix thoroughly.
3. Put in the buttermilk, cream, eggs and brandy.
4. Fold in the dry ingredients and mix thoroughly.
5. Put in the raspberries and pour the batter in a 9-inch round cake pan coated with baking paper.
6. Pre-heat the oven and bake at 350F for 50 minutes.
7. Let the cake cool in the pan and serve, sliced.

Nutritional Content of One Serving:

Calories: 415 Fat: 21.8g Protein: 5.6g Carbohydrates: 52.5g

Raspberry Ganache Cake

Total Time Taken: 1 ¼ hours
Yield: 8 Servings
Ingredients:

Cake:

- ¼ teaspoon salt

- ½ cup butter, softened
- ½ cup white sugar
- 1 cup all-purpose flour
- 1 cup fresh raspberries
- 1 teaspoon baking powder
- 4 eggs

Ganache:

- ½ cup heavy cream
- 1 cup dark chocolate chips

Directions:

1. For the cake, combine the butter and sugar in a container until fluffy. Put in the eggs, one at a time, then mix in the flour, salt and baking powder.
2. Spoon the batter in a 8-inch round cake pan coated with baking paper.
3. Top with raspberries and preheat your oven and bake at 350F for around forty minutes or until it rises significantly and starts to appear golden-brown.
4. Let the cake cool in the pan then move to a platter.
5. For the ganache, bring the cream to the boiling point in a saucepan. Turn off the heat and mix in the chocolate. Combine until melted.
6. Sprinkle the ganache over the cake and serve the cake chilled.

Nutritional Content of One Serving:

Calories: 341 Fat: 20.7g Protein: 5.8g Carbohydrates: 37.0g

Raspberry Lemon Olive Oil Cake

Total Time Taken: 1 hour
Yield: 10 Servings
Ingredients:

- ¼ cup butter, softened
- ¼ cup whole milk
- ¼ teaspoon baking soda
- ½ teaspoon salt
- ¾ cup extra virgin olive oil
- 1 ¾ cups all-purpose flour
- 1 cup fresh raspberries
- 1 cup white sugar
- 1 teaspoon baking powder
- 2 tablespoons lemon zest
- 4 eggs

Directions:

1. Mix the flour, baking powder, baking soda and salt in a container or platter.
2. In a separate container, mix the oil, butter and sugar and mix thoroughly. Stir in the eggs, one at a time, then put in the milk and lemon zest.

3. Fold in the dry ingredients then put in the raspberries.
4. Spoon the batter in a round cake pan coated with baking paper and preheat your oven and bake at 350F for around forty minutes or until a toothpick inserted into the center of the cake comes out clean.

The cake tastes best chilled.

Nutritional Content of One Serving:

Calories: 361 Fat: 22.0g Protein: 4.9g Carbohydrates: 39.1g

Raspberry Matcha Cake

Total Time Taken: 1 ¼ hours
 Yield: 10 Servings

Ingredients:

- ½ teaspoon salt
- 1 ½ cups all-purpose flour
- 1 cup fresh raspberries
- 1 tablespoons matcha powder
- 1 teaspoon vanilla extract
- 2 teaspoons baking powder
- 2/3 cup butter, softened
- 2/3 cup white sugar
- 4 eggs

Directions:

1. Sift the flour, matcha powder, baking powder and salt in a container.
2. Mix the butter and sugar until fluffy and creamy.
3. Put in the eggs, one at a time, and mix thoroughly after each addition. Stir in the vanilla then fold in the flour.
4. Put in the raspberries then spoon the batter in a loaf cake pan coated with baking paper.
5. Pre-heat the oven and bake at 350F for around forty minutes or until a toothpick inserted into the center of the cake comes out clean.
6. *The cake tastes best chilled.*

Nutritional Content of One Serving:

Calories: 262 Fat: 14.3g Protein: 4.4g Carbohydrates: 30.3g

Raspberry Ricotta Cake

Total Time Taken: 1 hour
 Yield: 10 Servings
Ingredients:

- ¼ cup cocoa powder
- ¼ teaspoon salt
- ½ cup butter, softened
- ¾ cup white sugar
- 1 cup hot water

- 1 cup raspberries
- 1 cup ricotta cheese
- 2 cups all-purpose flour
- 2 teaspoons baking powder

Directions:

1. Mix the ricotta cheese, butter and sugar in a container until creamy.
2. Put in the water and mix thoroughly.
3. Fold in the flour, cocoa powder, baking powder and salt.
4. Put in the raspberries then spoon the batter in a 9-inch round cake pan coated with baking paper.
5. Pre-heat the oven and bake at 350F for forty minutes or until a toothpick inserted into the center of the cake comes out clean.
6. The cake tastes best chilled.

Nutritional Content of One Serving:

Calories: 275 Fat: 11.8g Protein: 6.0g Carbohydrates: 38.5g

Rhubarb Upside Down Cake

Total Time Taken: 1 ¼ hours
Yield: 10 Servings

Ingredients:

- ½ cup sour cream
- ½ cup white sugar
- ½ teaspoon salt
- ¾ cup butter, softened
- ¾ cup white sugar
- 1 ½ teaspoons baking powder
- 1 teaspoon vanilla extract
- 2 cups all-purpose flour
- 3 eggs
- 4 rhubarb stalks, peeled and sliced

Directions:

1. Position the stalks of rhubarb in a 9-inch round cake pan coated with baking paper.
2. Top with ½ cup white sugar.
3. Mix the butter with
4. 1 cup sugar until fluffy and pale.
5. Put in the eggs and sour cream and mix thoroughly.
6. Stir in the vanilla then fold in the flour, baking powder and salt.
7. Pour the batter in the pan and preheat your oven and bake at 350F for about forty minutes.
8. When finished, flip the cake upside down on a platter.

Nutritional Content of One Serving:

Calories: 357 Fat: 17.8g Protein: 4.9g Carbohydrates: 46.0g

Rich Vanilla Cake

Total Time Taken: 1 hour
Yield: 10 Servings
Ingredients:

- ½ teaspoon salt
- 1 cup butter, softened
- 1 cup white sugar
- 1 tablespoon vanilla extract
- 2 cups all-purpose flour
- 2 egg whites
- 2 teaspoons baking powder
- 6 egg yolks

Directions:

1. Mix the butter, sugar and vanilla in a container until fluffy and creamy.
2. Put in the egg yolks and whole eggs, one at a time, stirring thoroughly after each addition.
3. Fold in the flour, baking powder and salt then spoon the batter in a 9-inch round cake pan coated with baking paper.
4. Pre-heat the oven and bake at 350F for around forty minutes or until a toothpick inserted into the center of the cake comes out clean.
5. Let the cake cool in the pan before you serve.

Nutritional Content of One Serving:

Calories: 369 Fat: 21.4g Protein: 5.1g Carbohydrates: 40.1g

Rum Pineapple Upside Down Cake

Total Time Taken: 1 ¼ hours
Yield: 10 Servings
Ingredients:

- ¼ cup butter, melted
- ¼ cup light rum
- ¼ teaspoon salt
- 1 ½ teaspoons baking powder
- 1 can pineapple rings, drained
- 1 cup white sugar
- 2 cups all-purpose flour
- 4 eggs

Directions:

1. Position the pineapple rings at the bottom of a 9-inch round cake pan coated with baking paper.
2. Mix the eggs and sugar in a container until volume increases to twice what it was.
3. Stir in the rum and melted butter then fold in the flour, baking powder and salt.
4. Pour the batter over the pineapple and preheat your oven and bake at 350F for around forty minutes.

5. When finished, flip it over on a platter and let cool before you serve.

Nutritional Content of One Serving:
Calories: 254 Fat: 6.6g Protein: 4.9g Carbohydrates: 41.7g

Snickerdoodle Bundt Cake

Total Time Taken: 1 ½ hours
Yield: 12 Servings
Ingredients:
Filling:
- 1 cup white sugar
- 1 tablespoon cinnamon powder

Cake:
- ½ teaspoon baking soda
- ½ teaspoon salt
- 1 cup butter, softened
- 1 cup sour cream
- 1 cup white sugar
- 1 teaspoon baking powder
- 1 teaspoon ground ginger
- 2 ½ cups all-purpose flour
- 2 tablespoons dark brown sugar
- 3 eggs

Directions:
1. For the filling, combine the sugar with cinnamon in a container.
2. For the cake, sift the flour, ginger, baking powder, baking soda and salt.
3. Mix the butter and sugars in a container until fluffy and light.
4. Put in the eggs, one at a time, then mix in the sour cream.
5. Fold in the flour then spoon half of the batter in a greased Bundt cake pan. Drizzle with the cinnamon sugar mixture then top with the rest of the batter.
6. Pre-heat the oven and bake at 350F for about forty-five minutes or until a golden-brown colour is achieved and a toothpick inserted into the center of the cake comes out clean.
7. *The cake tastes best chilled.*

Nutritional Content of One Serving:
Calories: 419 Fat: 20.7g Protein: 4.9g Carbohydrates: 55.9g

Sour Cherry Chocolate Cake

Total Time Taken: 1 ¼ hours
Yield: 10 Servings
Ingredients:
- ¼ cup whole milk
- ½ cup cocoa powder

- ½ teaspoon salt
- 1 cup all-purpose flour
- 1 cup butter, softened
- 1 cup heavy cream, whipped
- 1 cup sour cherries, pitted
- 1 cup white sugar
- 1 teaspoon baking powder
- 1 teaspoon vanilla extract
- 4 eggs

Directions:

1. Sift the flour with cocoa, salt and baking powder.
2. Mix the butter with sugar and vanilla until creamy. Put in the eggs, one at a time, then fold in the flour mixture.
3. Put in the cherries then spoon the batter in a 9-inch round cake pan coated with baking paper.
4. Pre-heat the oven and bake at 350F for around forty minutes or until a toothpick comes out clean after being inserted into the center of the cake.
5. Let the cake cool then move to a platter and cover it in whipped cream.
6. Serve fresh or place in your refrigerator.

Nutritional Content of One Serving:

Calories: 373 Fat: 25.5g Protein: 5.0g Carbohydrates: 35.0g

Spiced Pumpkin Sheet Cake

Total Time Taken: 1 ¼ hours
Yield: 16 Servings

Ingredients:

- ¼ teaspoon baking soda
- ½ cup walnuts, chopped
- ½ teaspoon ground cloves
- ½ teaspoon ground star anise
- ½ teaspoon salt
- 1 ½ cups pumpkin puree
- 1 ½ cups white sugar
- 1 cup canola oil
- 1 teaspoon cinnamon powder
- 1 teaspoon ground ginger
- 2 cups all-purpose flour
- 2 teaspoons baking powder
- 4 eggs

Directions:

1. Sift the flour, baking powder, baking soda, salt and spices in a container.
2. Mix the sugar, canola oil and eggs in a container until pale and fluffy.

3. Stir in the pumpkin puree then incorporate the flour, ½ cup at a time, mixing gently using a spatula.
4. Fold in the walnuts then spoon the batter in a 10x10 inch rectangle pan coated with baking paper.
5. Pre-heat the oven and bake at 350F for around forty minutes or until a toothpick inserted into the center of the cake comes out clean.
6. The cake tastes best chilled, cut into small squares.

Nutritional Content of One Serving:
Calories: 297 Fat: 17.3g Protein: 4.2g Carbohydrates: 33.5g

Spiced Walnut Cake

Total Time Taken: 1 hour
Yield: 8 Servings
Ingredients:

3 eggs
- ¼ cup canola oil
- ½ teaspoon ground cardamom
- ½ teaspoon ground ginger
- ½ teaspoon salt
- ¾ cup all-purpose flour
- 1 cup ground walnuts
- 1 cup white sugar
- 1 teaspoon baking soda
- 1 teaspoon cinnamon powder

Directions:
1. Mix the eggs and sugar in a container until fluffy and volume increases to twice what it was.
2. Stir in the canola oil then fold in the walnuts, cinnamon, ginger, cardamom, flour, salt and baking soda.
3. Pour the batter in a 8-inch round cake pan coated with baking paper.
4. Pre-heat the oven and bake at 350F for around forty minutes or until it rises completely and is aromatic.
5. Let the cake cool in the pan and serve, sliced.

Nutritional Content of One Serving:
Calories: 318 Fat: 17.8g Protein: 7.1g Carbohydrates: 35.8g

Pumpkin Nutella Muffins

Total Time Taken: 1 hour
Yield: 12 Servings
Ingredients:
- ¼ teaspoon salt
- ½ cup coconut oil, melted
- ½ cup Nutella
- ½ teaspoon ground ginger
- ½ teaspoon ground nutmeg
- 1 ½ cups pumpkin puree

- 1 cup white sugar
- 1 teaspoon baking powder
- 1 teaspoon baking soda
- 1 teaspoon cinnamon powder
- 1 teaspoon vanilla extract
- 2 cups all-purpose flour
- 2 eggs

Directions:

1. Mix the flour, sugar, baking powder, baking soda, salt, cinnamon, nutmeg and ginger.
2. Put in the eggs, vanilla, pumpkin puree and coconut oil and stir for a few seconds to mix.
3. Spoon the batter in a muffin tin covered with muffin papers.
4. Drop a spoonful of Nutella on top of each muffin then swirl it with a toothpick.
5. Pre-heat the oven and bake at 350F for about twenty minutes or until it rises significantly and starts to appear golden-brown.

These muffins taste best chilled.

Nutritional Content of One Serving:

Calories: 256 Fat: 11.1g Protein: 3.6g Carbohydrates: 37.2g

Pumpkin Pecan Crunch Muffins

Total Time Taken: 1 ¼ hours
Yield: 12 Servings
Ingredients:

Muffins:

- ¼ cup butter, chilled
- ¼ teaspoon salt
- ½ cup all-purpose flour
- ½ cup coconut milk Pecan crunch:
- ½ cup coconut oil, melted
- ½ cup ground pecans
- ½ cup light brown sugar
- ½ cup pecans, chopped
- 1 ½ cups all-purpose flour
- 1 cup pumpkin puree
- 1 teaspoon baking soda
- 1 teaspoon pumpkin pie spices
- 2 eggs
- 2 tablespoons light brown sugar

Directions:

1. For the muffins, combine the dry ingredients in a container.
2. Put in the remaining ingredients, all at once, and stir for a few seconds to mix just until incorporated.
3. Spoon the batter in a muffin tin coated with baking muffin papers.

4. For the pecan crunch, combine the ingredients in a container until sandy.
5. Spread the crunch over the muffins and preheat your oven and bake at 350F for about twenty minutes or until the top is crunchy and golden brown.
6. Let cool in the pan before you serve.

Nutritional Content of One Serving:

Calories: 274 Fat: 18.0g Protein: 3.8g Carbohydrates: 26.0g

Pure Vanilla Muffins

Total Time Taken: 1 hour
Yield: 10 Servings
Ingredients:

- ¼ cup sour cream
- ½ cup canola oil
- ½ cup white sugar
- ½ teaspoon salt
- 1 ½ cups all-purpose flour
- 1 teaspoon baking powder
- 1 teaspoon vanilla extract
- 2 eggs

Directions:

1. Mix the eggs and sugar in a container until pale and light.
2. Put in the canola oil, vanilla and sour cream and mix thoroughly.
3. Fold in the flour, salt and baking powder then spoon the batter in a muffin tin covered with muffin papers.
4. Pre-heat the oven and bake at 350F for about twenty minutes or until it rises significantly and seems golden.

These muffins taste best chilled.

Nutritional Content of One Serving:

Calories: 229 Fat: 13.2g Protein: 3.2g Carbohydrates: 24.9g

Quick Coffee Muffins

Total Time Taken: 1 hour
Yield: 12 Servings
Ingredients:

- ¼ cup brewed espresso
- ¼ teaspoon salt
- ½ cup canola oil
- ½ cup hot water
- ½ teaspoon baking soda
- ¾ cup cocoa powder
- 1 ½ cups white sugar
- 1 ¾ cups all-purpose flour

- 1 cup buttermilk
- 1 teaspoon baking powder
- 1 teaspoon vanilla extract
- 2 eggs

Directions:

1. Mix the dry ingredients in a container.
2. Put in the remaining ingredients and stir for a few seconds to mix.
3. Pour the batter in a muffin tin covered with muffin papers and preheat your oven and bake at 350F for about twenty minutes or until a toothpick inserted into them comes out dry.
4. *Let cool down before you serve.*

Nutritional Content of One Serving:

Calories: 277 Fat: 10.9g Protein: 4.6g Carbohydrates: 44.1g

Quinoa Cranberry Muffins

Total Time Taken: 1 hour
Yield: 12 Servings
Ingredients:

- ¼ cup all-purpose flour
- ¼ cup butter, melted
- ¼ cup white sugar
- ¼ teaspoon salt
- ½ cup quinoa flour
- 1 cup cranberries
- 1 cup plain yogurt
- 1 cup whole wheat flour
- 2 eggs
- 2 tablespoons sunflower seeds
- 2 teaspoons baking powder

Directions:

1. Mix the flours, salt, baking powder, sunflower seeds in a container.
2. Put in the yogurt, eggs, sugar and butter and stir for a few seconds to mix.
3. Fold in the cranberries then spoon the batter in a muffin tin coated with baking muffin papers.
4. Pre-heat the oven and bake at 350F for about twenty minutes or until it rises significantly and seems golden.
5. *Let cool down before you serve.*

Nutritional Content of One Serving:

Calories: 149 Fat: 5.7g Protein: 5.2g Carbohydrates: 18.1g

Quinoa Peach Muffins

Total Time Taken: 1 hour
Yield: 12 Servings
Ingredients:

- 2 cups all-purpose flour
- 1 teaspoon vanilla extract
- 1 teaspoon baking powder
- 1 egg
- 1 cup cooked quinoa
- 1 cup buttermilk
- ¾ cups light brown sugar
- ½ teaspoon baking soda
- ¼ teaspoon salt
- ¼ cup canola oil

Directions:

1. Mix the quinoa, canola oil, egg, buttermilk and vanilla in a container.
2. Stir in the sugar and mix thoroughly then put in the flour, salt, baking powder and baking soda.
3. Spoon the batter in a muffin tin covered with muffin papers.
4. Pre-heat the oven and bake at 350F for about twenty minutes or until well risen.
5. *Let cool down before you serve.*

Nutritional Content of One Serving:
Calories: 217 Fat: 6.1g Protein: 5.3g Carbohydrates: 35.1g

Almond Blueberry Cookies

Total Time Taken: 1 ¼ hours
Yield: 20 Servings
Ingredients:

- ½ cup butter, softened
- 1 teaspoon lemon zest
- 1 egg
- ¼ cup whole milk
- 1 teaspoon almond extract
- 1 ¼ cups all-purpose flour
- 1 cup ground almonds
- ¼ teaspoon salt
- ½ teaspoon baking soda
- ½ cup dried blueberries
- ¼ cup sliced almonds
- 2/3 cup white sugar

Directions:

1. Mix the butter, sugar and lemon zest in a container until fluffy and pale.
2. Put in the egg and milk and mix thoroughly then fold in the flour, ground almonds, baking soda, salt and blueberries.
3. Drop spoonfuls of batter on a baking tray covered with parchment paper and top each cookie with almond slices.
4. Preheat your oven and bake the cookies at 350F for about fifteen minutes or until a golden-brown colour is achieved and fragrant.
5. Serve Chilled or store them in an airtight container for maximum 1 week.

Nutritional Content of One Serving:
Calories: 136 Fat: 8.0g Protein: 2.5g Carbohydrates: 14.6g

Almond Cookies

Total Time Taken: 1 ¼ hours
Yield: 20 Servings

Ingredients:

- ½ cup butter, softened
- 1 teaspoon almond extract
- 2 egg yolks
- 1 ½ cups all-purpose flour
- ½ cup almond flour
- ¼ teaspoon salt
- 1 teaspoon baking powder
- ½ cup sliced almonds
- 2/3 cup white sugar

Directions:

1. Mix the butter, sugar and almond extract in a container until fluffy and pale.
2. Put in the egg yolks and stir thoroughly until blended.
3. Fold in the flours, salt and baking powder.
4. Drop spoonfuls of batter on a baking sheet coated with baking paper.
5. Top each cookie with sliced almonds and preheat your oven and bake at 350F for about fifteen minutes until a golden-brown colour is achieved on the edges.
6. These cookies taste best chilled.

Nutritional Content of One Serving:
Calories: 124 Fat: 6.7g Protein: 1.9g Carbohydrates: 14.7g

Amaretti Cookies

Total Time Taken: 1 ¼ hours
Yield: 10 Servings

Ingredients:

- ¼ cup all-purpose flour
- ¼ teaspoon salt 2 egg whites
- ½ cup light brown sugar

- ½ teaspoon baking powder
- 1 teaspoon vanilla extract
- 2 cups almond flour

Directions:

1. Whip the egg whites with salt and vanilla in a container until fluffy.
2. Put in the sugar and continue mixing until shiny and firm.
3. Drop spoonfuls of batter on a baking tray coated with baking paper.
4. Pre-heat the oven and bake at 350F for about twenty minutes or until a golden-brown colour is achieved and crisp.
5. *These cookies taste best chilled.*

Nutritional Content of One Serving:

Calories: 76 Fat: 2.8g Protein: 2.2g Carbohydrates: 10.9g

Amaretti Cookies

Total Time Taken: 1 hour
Yield: 10 Servings
Ingredients:

- 2 cups almond flour
- 1 teaspoon vanilla extract
- ½ teaspoon almond extract
- 2 egg whites
- 2/3 cup light brown sugar

Directions:

1. Mix the egg whites until fluffy.
2. Put in the vanilla and sugar and continue whipping until shiny and firm.
3. Fold in the almond flour then drop spoonfuls of batter on a baking tray coated with baking paper.
4. Preheat your oven and bake the cookies at 350F for about fifteen minutes or until a golden-brown colour is achieved on the edges.
5. These cookies taste best chilled.

Nutritional Content of One Serving:

Calories: 74 Fat: 2.8g Protein: 1.9g Carbohydrates: 10.8g

American Chocolate Chunk Cookies

Total Time Taken: 1 ¼ hours
Yield: 20 Servings
Ingredients:

- ½ cup smooth peanut butter
- ½ cup light brown sugar
- 1 egg
- 1 teaspoon vanilla extract
- 1 cup all-purpose flour

- ¼ teaspoon salt
- ½ teaspoon baking powder
- ½ cup peanuts, chopped
- 3 oz. dark chocolate, chopped
- 1/3 cup butter, softened

Directions:

1. Mix the peanut butter, butter and sugar in a container until fluffy and creamy.
2. Put in the egg and vanilla and mix thoroughly.
3. Fold in the flour, salt, baking powder, peanuts and dark chocolate.
4. Drop spoonfuls of batter on a baking tray coated with baking paper.
5. Preheat your oven and bake the cookies at 350F for about fifteen minutes or until a golden-brown colour is achieved on the edges.
    6. *These cookies taste best chilled.*

Nutritional Content of One Serving:

Calories: 149 Fat: 9.7g Protein: 3.9g Carbohydrates: 12.8g

Anzac Cookies

Total Time Taken: 1 ¼ hours
Yield: 20 Servings

Ingredients:

- ¼ teaspoon salt
- ½ cup shredded coconut
- ½ teaspoon baking soda
- ¾ cup all-purpose flour
- ¾ cup butter, melted
- 1 cup rolled oats
- 1 teaspoon lemon juice
- 4 tablespoons golden syrup

Directions:

1. Mix the oats, coconut, flour, baking soda and salt in a container.
2. Put in the rest of the ingredients and mix thoroughly.
3. Make small balls of dough and place them in a baking tray coated with baking paper.
4. Flatten the cookies slightly then preheat your oven and bake at 350F for about fifteen minutes or until a golden-brown colour is achieved on the edges.
5. *These cookies taste best chilled.*

Nutritional Content of One Serving:

Calories: 112 Fat: 7.9g Protein: 1.2g Carbohydrates: 9.8g

Apricot Coconut Cookies

Total Time Taken: 1 ½ hours
Yield: 25 Servings

Ingredients:

- ¼ cup light brown sugar
- ¼ teaspoon salt
- ½ cup butter, softened
- ½ cup dark chocolate chips
- ½ cup dried apricots, chopped
- ½ cup rolled oats
- ½ cup white sugar
- ½ teaspoon baking soda
- 1 cup all-purpose flour
- 1 cup shredded coconut
- 1 teaspoon vanilla extract
- 2 eggs

Directions:

1. Mix the flour, coconut, oats, apricots, salt and baking soda in a container.
2. In a separate container, mix the butter and the sugars and vanilla and mix thoroughly.
3. Fold in the flour mixture and the chocolate chips.
4. Drop spoonful of batter on a baking sheet coated with baking paper.
5. Pre-heat the oven and bake at 350F for about fifteen minutes or until a golden-brown colour is achieved on the edges.
6. Let the cookies cool before you serve.

Nutritional Content of One Serving:

Calories: 107 Fat: 5.9g Protein: 1.5g Carbohydrates: 12.8g

Banana Chocolate Chip Cookies

Total Time Taken: 1 ¼ hours
Yield: 20 Servings

Ingredients:

- ¼ teaspoon salt
- ½ cup butter, melted
- ½ cup dark chocolate chips
- ½ cup white sugar
- 1 ½ cups all-purpose flour
- 1 egg
- 1 teaspoon baking powder
- 1 teaspoon vanilla extract
- 2 bananas, mashed

Directions:

1. Combine all the dry ingredients in a container.
2. Put in the rest of the ingredients and mix thoroughly using a spatula.
3. Drop spoonfuls of batter on a baking tray covered with parchment paper.

4. Preheat your oven and bake the cookies at 350F for about fifteen minutes or until a golden-brown colour is achieved on the edges.
5. *These cookies taste best chilled.*

Nutritional Content of One Serving:
Calories: 122 Fat: 5.8g Protein: 1.6g Carbohydrates: 17.0g

Banana Chocolate Cookies

Total Time Taken: 1 ¼ hours
Yield: 20 Servings
Ingredients:

- ¼ cup butter, softened
- ¼ cup cocoa powder
- ¼ cup coconut oil, melted
- ¼ teaspoon baking soda
- ¼ teaspoon salt
- ½ cup walnuts, chopped
- ½ teaspoon baking powder
- 1 ¾ cups all-purpose flour
- 2 bananas, mashed
- 2/3 cup white sugar

Directions:

1. **Mix** the butter, oil and sugar in a container until creamy and fluffy.
2. **Stir in** the bananas then fold in the flour, baking soda, baking powder, salt and cocoa powder.
3. Put in the walnuts then drop spoonfuls of batter on a baking sheet **coated with baking paper** .
4. **Preheat your oven and bake the cookies at** 350F for **fifteen minutes** or **until aromatic** .
5. **These cookies taste best chilled** .

Nutritional Content of One Serving:
Calories: 141 Fat: 7.2g Protein: 2.2g Carbohydrates: 18.7g

Banana Oatmeal Cookies

Total Time Taken: 1 hour
Yield: 10 Servings
Ingredients:

- ¼ teaspoon baking soda
- 1 cup rolled oats
- 1 pinch salt
- 2 tablespoons maple syrup
- 3 ripe bananas, mashed

Directions:

1. Combine all the ingredients in a container.
2. Drop spoonfuls of batter on a baking sheet coated with baking paper.

3. Preheat your oven and bake the cookies at 350F for about ten minutes or until a golden-brown colour is achieved on the edges.
4. *These cookies taste best chilled.*

Nutritional Content of One Serving:

Calories: 73 Fat: 0.7g Protein: 1.5g Carbohydrates: 16.3g

Brown Butter American Cookies

Total Time Taken: 1 ¼ hours
Yield: 20 Servings

Ingredients:

- ¼ teaspoon salt
- ½ cup pecans, chopped
- ½ teaspoon baking soda
- 1 ½ cups all-purpose flour
- 1 cup butter
- 1 cup light brown sugar
- 1 egg
- 1 teaspoon vanilla extract

Directions:

1. Put the butter in a saucepan and melt it then cook it until golden and caramelized. Let cool and then move to a container.
2. Mix the butter and sugar in a fluffy and pale.
3. Put in the egg and vanilla and mix thoroughly then mix in the flour, baking soda, salt and pecans.
4. Drop spoonfuls of batter on a baking tray coated with baking paper.
5. Pre-heat the oven and bake at 350F for about fifteen minutes or until a golden-brown colour is achieved on the edges.
6. *These cookies taste best chilled.*

Nutritional Content of One Serving:

Calories: 152 Fat: 10.0g Protein: 1.4g Carbohydrates: 14.4g

Brown Butter Chocolate Chip Cookies

Total Time Taken: 2 hours
Yield: 20 Servings
Ingredients:

- ¼ teaspoon salt
- ½ cup butter
- ½ teaspoon baking soda
- 1 ½ cups all-purpose flour
- 1 cup dark chocolate chips
- 1 cup light brown sugar
- 1 egg

- 1 egg yolk
- 1 teaspoon baking powder
- 1 teaspoon vanilla extract

Directions:

1. Mix the flour, baking powder, baking soda and salt in a container.
2. Melt the butter in a saucepan until it starts to appear somewhat golden-brown and caramelized. Let cool and then move to a container.
3. Stir in the sugar, egg, egg yolk, vanilla and flour. Stir slowly until mixed using a spatula.
4. Fold in the chocolate chips then drop spoonfuls of dough on a baking sheet coated with baking paper.
5. Freeze the cookies for about half an hour then preheat your oven and bake at 350F for fifteen minutes until a golden-brown colour is achieved.

Best served chilled.

Nutritional Content of One Serving:

Calories: 137 Fat: 6.8g Protein: 1.8g Carbohydrates: 18.5g

Brown Butter Chocolate Oatmeal Cookies

Total Time Taken: 1 ¼ hours
Yield: 30 Servings

Ingredients:

- ¼ teaspoon salt
- ½ cup dark chocolate chips
- 1 1/2 cups rolled oats
- 1 cup all-purpose flour
- 1 cup butter
- 1 cup light brown sugar
- 1 egg
- 1 teaspoon baking soda
- 1 teaspoon vanilla extract

Directions:

1. Melt the butter in a saucepan until it becomes mildly golden.
2. Put in the sugar and mix thoroughly then mix in the egg and vanilla.
3. Put in the oats, flour, baking soda and salt then fold in the chocolate chips.
4. Drop spoonfuls of batter on a baking tray coated with baking paper.
5. Preheat your oven and bake the cookies at 350F for about fifteen minutes or until a golden-brown colour is achieved on the edges.
6. *These cookies taste best chilled.*

Nutritional Content of One Serving:

Calories: 115 Fat: 7.1g Protein: 1.4g Carbohydrates: 12.0g

Brown Sugar Chocolate Chip Cookies

Total Time Taken: 1 ½ hours
Yield: 40 Servings

Ingredients:

- ½ cup white sugar
- ½ teaspoon salt
- 1 ½ cups butter, softened
- 1 ½ cups dark chocolate chips
- 1 cup dark brown sugar
- 1 cup light brown sugar
- 1 teaspoon baking soda
- 1 teaspoon vanilla extract
- 2 eggs
- 3 cups all-purpose flour

Directions:

1. Mix the butter and sugars in a container until creamy and fluffy.
2. Put in the eggs and vanilla and mix thoroughly then fold in the remaining ingredients.
3. Drop spoonfuls of batter on a baking tray coated with baking paper.
4. Preheat your oven and bake the cookies at 350F for about fifteen minutes or until a golden-brown colour is achieved on the edges and crisp.
5. *These cookies taste best chilled.*

Nutritional Content of One Serving:
Calories: 157 Fat: 8.4g Protein: 1.6g Carbohydrates: 19.8g

Butter Vanilla Cookies

Total Time Taken: 1 hour
Yield: 30 Servings
Ingredients:

- ¼ cup cornstarch
- ¼ teaspoon salt
- ½ cup powdered sugar
- 1 cup butter, softened
- 1 egg
- 1 tablespoon vanilla extract
- 2 cups all-purpose flour

Directions:

1. Mix the butter and sugar in a container until fluffy and creamy.
2. Put in the egg and vanilla and mix thoroughly.
3. Fold in the flour, cornstarch and salt and mix thoroughly.
4. Drop spoonfuls of batter on a baking sheet coated with baking paper.
5. Pre-heat the oven and bake at 350F for about fifteen minutes or until a golden-brown colour is achieved on the edges.
6. *These cookies taste best chilled.*

Nutritional Content of One Serving:

Calories: 100 Fat: 6.4g Protein: 1.1g Carbohydrates: 9.4g

Cakey Chocolate Chip Cookies

Total Time Taken: 1 hour
Yield: 20 Servings
Ingredients:

- ¼ cup coconut oil, melted
- ¼ cup whole milk
- ¼ teaspoon salt
- ½ cup dark chocolate chips
- ½ cup white sugar
- ½ teaspoon baking powder
- 1 ½ cups all-purpose flour
- 1 egg

Directions:

1. Mix the egg and sugar in a container until volume increases to twice what it was.
2. Put in the coconut oil and milk and mix thoroughly.
3. Stir in the remaining ingredients then drop spoonfuls of batter on a baking tray coated with baking paper.
4. Preheat your oven and bake the cookies at 350F for about ten minutes or until it rises and appears golden.
5. Let cool in the pan before you serve.

Nutritional Content of One Serving:
Calories: 96 Fat: 3.9g Protein: 1.6g Carbohydrates: 14.4g

Candied Ginger Oatmeal Cookies

Total Time Taken: 1 hour
Yield: 30 Servings
Ingredients:

- ¼ cup butter, softened
- ½ cup candied ginger, chopped
- ½ cup canola oil
- ½ teaspoon salt
- 1 cup light brown sugar
- 1 teaspoon baking soda
- 1 teaspoon vanilla extract
- 2 cups all-purpose flour
- 2 cups rolled oats
- 2 eggs

Directions:

1. Mix the butter and sugar in a container until creamy and pale.

2. Put in the eggs and mix thoroughly then mix in the vanilla.
3. Fold in the dry ingredients and ginger then drop spoonfuls of batter on a baking sheet coated with baking paper.
4. Preheat your oven and bake the cookies at 350F for about fifteen minutes or until it is aromatic and appears golden-brown on the edges.
5. *These cookies taste best chilled.*

Nutritional Content of One Serving:
Calories: 121 Fat: 5.9g Protein: 2.0g Carbohydrates: 15.0g

Candy Cane Chocolate Cookies

Total Time Taken: 1 ¼ hours
Yield: 20 Servings
Ingredients:

- ¼ cup cocoa powder
- ¼ cup shredded coconut
- ¼ teaspoon salt
- ½ cup butter, softened
- ½ cup crushed candy cane cookies
- ½ teaspoon baking soda
- 1 cup all-purpose flour
- 1 egg
- 1 teaspoon vanilla extract
- 2 tablespoons canola oil
- 2/3 cup light brown sugar

Directions:

1. Mix the butter, canola oil, sugar and vanilla in a container until fluffy and creamy.
2. Stir in the egg then put in the flour, cocoa powder, coconut, baking soda and salt.
3. Fold in the crushed candy then drop spoonfuls of batter on a baking sheet coated with baking paper.
4. Preheat your oven and bake the cookies at 350F for about fifteen minutes or until aromatic and risen.
5. *These cookies taste best chilled.*

Nutritional Content of One Serving:
Calories: 108 Fat: 7.0g Protein: 1.3g Carbohydrates: 10.8g

Cardamom Chocolate Chip Cookies

Total Time Taken: 1 hour
Yield: 20 Servings
Ingredients:

- ½ cup light brown sugar
- ½ cup white sugar
- ½ teaspoon salt
- 1 cup butter, softened

- 1 cup dark chocolate chips
- 1 teaspoon baking powder
- 1 teaspoon cardamom powder
- 2 ½ cups all-purpose flour
- 2 eggs

Directions:

1. Mix the butter and sugars in a container until creamy and fluffy.
2. Stir in the eggs, one at a time, then put in the flour, salt, baking powder and cardamom powder.
3. Fold in the chocolate chips then drop spoonfuls of batter on a baking sheet coated with baking paper.
4. Pre-heat the oven and bake at 350F for about fifteen minutes.
5. Let the cookies cool in the pan before you serve.

Nutritional Content of One Serving:

Calories: 206 Fat: 11.4g Protein: 2.7g Carbohydrates: 24.7g

Cashew Cranberry Cookies

Total Time Taken: 1 ¼ house
Yield: 30 Servings

Ingredients:

- ¼ teaspoon salt
- ½ cup all-purpose flour
- ½ cup baking soda
- ½ cup coconut oil, melted
- ½ cup light brown sugar
- 1 ½ cups ground cashew nuts
- 1 cup dried cranberries
- 1 teaspoon vanilla extract
- 2 eggs
- 2 tablespoons golden syrup

Directions:

1. Mix the cashew nuts, flour, salt and baking soda in a container.
2. In a separate container, combine the coconut oil, eggs, vanilla, sugar and syrup until creamy.
3. Put in the flour mixture then fold in the cranberries.
4. Drop spoonfuls of batter on a baking sheet coated with baking paper.
5. Preheat your oven and bake the cookies at 350F for about fifteen minutes or until a golden-brown colour is achieved on the edges.
6. *These cookies taste best chilled.*

Nutritional Content of One Serving:

Calories: 106 Fat: 7.7g Protein: 2.0g Carbohydrates: 7.6g

Chewy Coconut Cookies

Total Time Taken: 1 hour
Yield: 20 Servings
Ingredients:

- ¼ cup coconut oil, melted
- ¼ cup cornstarch
- ¼ teaspoon salt
- ½ teaspoon baking soda
- ½ teaspoon coconut extract
- 1 ¼ cups all-purpose flour
- 1 cup shredded coconut
- 1 cup white sugar
- 1 egg
- 1 teaspoon vanilla extract

Directions:

1. Mix the egg and sugar in a container until volume increases to twice what it was. Stir in the coconut oil then put in the coconut oil, vanilla and coconut extract.
2. Fold in the flour, cornstarch, baking soda, salt and coconut.
3. Drop spoonfuls of batter on a baking sheet pan coated with baking paper.
4. Preheat your oven and bake the cookies at 350F for about fifteen minutes or until a golden-brown colour is achieved on the edges.
5. *These cookies taste best chilled.*

Nutritional Content of One Serving:

Calories: 114 Fat: 4.4g Protein: 1.2g Carbohydrates: 18.1g

Chewy Sugar Cookies

Total Time Taken: 1 ¼ hours
Yield: 40 Servings
Ingredients:

- ½ teaspoon salt
- 1 cup butter, softened
- 1 teaspoon baking soda
- 1 teaspoon vanilla extract
- 2 ½ cups all-purpose flour
- 2 cups white sugar
- 2 eggs

Directions:

1. Mix the butter with sugar until creamy and pale. Put in the eggs, one at a time, then mix in the vanilla.
2. Fold in the flour, baking soda and salt then shape the dough into small balls.
3. Put the balls on a baking tray coated with baking paper and flatten them slightly.

4. Preheat your oven and bake the cookies at 350F for about fifteen minutes or until mildly golden brown.
5. *These cookies taste best chilled.*

Nutritional Content of One Serving:
Calories: 110 Fat: 4.9g Protein: 1.1g Carbohydrates: 16.0g

Chili Chocolate Cookies

Total Time Taken: 1 ¼ hours
Yield: 30 Servings
Ingredients:

- ¼ cup dark brown sugar
- ½ cup cocoa powder
- ½ cup white sugar
- ½ teaspoon salt
- 1 cup butter, softened
- 1 cup dark chocolate chips
- 1 teaspoon baking powder
- 1 teaspoon chili powder
- 1 teaspoon vanilla extract
- 2 cups all-purpose flour
- 2 eggs

Directions:

1. Mix the butter and sugars in a container until creamy and fluffy.
2. Put in the vanilla and eggs and mix thoroughly.
3. Fold in the flour, cocoa powder, salt, chili powder and baking powder then put in the chocolate chips.
4. Drop spoonfuls of batter on a baking sheet coated with baking paper.
5. Preheat your oven and bake the cookies at 350F for about fifteen minutes or until risen and fragrant.
6. *These cookies taste best chilled.*

Nutritional Content of One Serving:
Calories: 129 Fat: 7.8g Protein: 1.8g Carbohydrates: 14.5g

Chocolate Buttercream Cookies

Total Time Taken: 1 ½ hours
Yield: 20 Servings
Ingredients:
Cookies:

- ½ cup butter, softened
- ½ cup cocoa powder
- ½ cup coconut oil
- ½ cup powdered sugar
- ½ teaspoon baking powder
- ½ teaspoon salt

- 1 egg
- 2 cups all-purpose flour
- 2 tablespoons whole milk

Filling:

- ½ cup butter, softened
- 1 cup powdered sugar

Directions:

1. For the cookies, combine the flour, cocoa powder, salt and baking powder in a container.
2. In a separate container, combine the coconut oil, butter and sugar in a container until creamy and fluffy.
3. Put in the egg and mix thoroughly, then mix in the flour and the milk.
4. Cover the dough with plastic wrap and store in the refrigerator for about half an hour.
5. Transfer the dough to a floured working surface and roll into a slim sheet.
6. Cut small round cookies and place them on a baking sheet.
7. Pre-heat the oven and bake at 350F for about fifteen minutes.
8. Let the cookies cool to room temperature.
9. For the filling, combine the butter with sugar until fluffy and creamy.
10. Fill the cookies, two by two with the buttercream.
11. Serve fresh or store in an airtight container.

Nutritional Content of One Serving:

Calories: 218 Fat: 15.4g Protein: 2.1g Carbohydrates: 19.8g

Chocolate Chip Pecan Cookies

Total Time Taken: 1 ¼ hours
Yield: 20 Servings

Ingredients:

- ¼ teaspoon salt
- ½ cup butter, softened
- ½ cup chocolate chips
- ½ cup powdered sugar
- ½ teaspoon baking soda
- 1 cup all-purpose flour
- 1 cup ground pecans
- 1 egg
- 2 tablespoon honey

Directions:

1. Mix the butter, sugar and honey in a container until creamy and pale.
2. Put in the egg and mix thoroughly then put in the flour, pecans, baking soda and salt.
3. Fold in the chocolate chips then drop spoonfuls of batter on a baking sheet coated with baking paper.
4. Pre-heat the oven and bake at 350F for about fifteen minutes or until a golden-brown colour is achieved and fragrant.
5. *These cookies taste best chilled.*

Chocolate Chunk Cookies

Total Time Taken: 1 ¼ hours
Yield: 20 Servings
Ingredients:

- ¼ teaspoon salt
- ½ cup butter, softened
- 1 ½ cups all-purpose flour
- 1 egg
- 1 teaspoon baking powder
- 2 tablespoons honey
- 2/3 cup light brown sugar
- 4 oz. dark chocolate, chopped

Directions:

1. Mix the butter, honey and sugar in a container until fluffy and pale.
2. Put in the egg and mix thoroughly then mix in the flour, baking powder and salt.
3. Fold in the chocolate then drop spoonfuls of dough on a baking sheet coated with baking paper.
4. Preheat your oven and bake the cookies at 350F for fifteen minutes or until a golden-brown colour is achieved on the edges.
5. *These cookies taste best chilled.*

Nutritional Content of One Serving:
Calories: 133 Fat: 6.6g Protein: 1.8g Carbohydrates: 17.1g

Chocolate Crinkles

Total Time Taken: 2 hours
Yield: 40 Servings
Ingredients:

- ½ cup cocoa powder
- ½ cup coconut oil, melted
- ½ teaspoon salt
- 1 ½ teaspoons baking powder
- 1 teaspoon vanilla extract
- 2 cups all-purpose flour
- 2 cups powdered sugar
- 2 cups white sugar
- 4 eggs
- 4 oz. dark chocolate, melted

Directions:

1. Mix the coconut oil and melted chocolate in a container.

2. Put in the sugar and eggs and mix thoroughly then mix in the vanilla.
3. Fold in the flour, baking powder, cocoa and salt then cover the dough using plastic wrap.
4. Place in your refrigerator for an hour then form small balls of dough and roll them through powdered sugar.
5. Put the cookies on a baking tray coated with baking paper and preheat your oven and bake at 350F for about ten minutes.
6. *These cookies taste best chilled.*

Nutritional Content of One Serving:
Calories: 131 Fat: 4.2g Protein: 1.6g Carbohydrates: 23.1g

Chocolate Dipped Sugar Cookies

Total Time Taken: 1 ¼ hours
Yield: 30 Servings

Ingredients:

- ¼ teaspoon salt
- 1 cup butter, softened
- 1 cup dark chocolate, melted
- 1 cup powdered sugar
- 1 teaspoon baking powder
- 1 teaspoon vanilla extract
- 2 egg yolks
- 3 cups all-purpose flour

Directions:

1. Mix the butter and sugar in a container until pale and fluffy.
2. Stir in the egg yolks and vanilla and mix thoroughly.
3. Fold in the flour, baking powder and salt then wrap the dough in plastic wrap and store in the refrigerator for about half an hour.
4. Transfer the dough to a floured working surface and roll into a slim sheet.
5. Cut cookies using a cookie cutter of your choices and arrange them on a baking sheet coated with baking paper.
6. Pre-heat the oven and bake at 350F for about thirteen minutes or until mildly golden-brown on the edges.
7. When finished, allow the cookies to cool then immerse them in melted chocolate.
8. *These cookies taste best chilled.*

Nutritional Content of One Serving:
Calories: 149 Fat: 8.2g Protein: 2.0g Carbohydrates: 17.0g

Chocolate Drizzled Lavender Cookies

Total Time Taken: 1 ½ hours
Yield: 20 Servings

Ingredients:

- ¼ cup cornstarch

- ¼ teaspoon baking soda
- ¼ teaspoon salt
- ½ cup butter, softened
- ½ cup powdered sugar
- ½ cup white chocolate chips, melted
- 1 ½ cups all-purpose flour
- 1 egg
- 1 egg yolk
- 1 teaspoon lavender buds
- 2 tablespoons whole milk

Directions:

1. Mix the butter with sugar in a container until fluffy and pale.
2. Stir in the egg and egg yolk and mix thoroughly.
3. Put in the milk and mix then fold in the remaining ingredients. Mix the dough then move it to a floured working surface and roll it into a slim sheet.
4. Cut into small cookies using a cookie cutter of your choices.
5. Position the cookies on a baking sheet coated with baking paper.
6. Pre-heat the oven and bake at 350F for about fifteen minutes or until a golden-brown colour is achieved on the edges.
7. When finished, let cool in the pan then sprinkle the cookies with melted chocolate.
8. **Best served chilled.**

Nutritional Content of One Serving:

Calories: 122 Fat: 6.6g Protein: 1.7g Carbohydrates: 14.2g

Chocolate Hazelnut Cookies

Total Time Taken: 1 ½ hours
Yield: 30 Servings

Ingredients:

- ¼ cup cocoa powder
- ¼ teaspoon salt
- ½ cup cream cheese, softened
- ½ cup ground hazelnuts
- 1 ½ cups all-purpose flour
- 1 cup butter, softened
- 1 egg yolk

Directions:

1. Mix the butter, cream cheese and egg yolk in a container until creamy.
2. Put in the salt, flour, cocoa powder and hazelnuts and mix using a spatula.
3. Wrap the plastic wrap and store in the refrigerator for about half an hour.
4. Transfer the dough to a floured working surface and roll it into a slim sheet.
5. Cut into small cookies with a cookie cutter of your choices.

6. Put the cookies in a baking sheet coated with baking paper and preheat your oven and bake at 350F for about ten minutes or until a golden-brown colour is achieved on the edges.
7. These cookies taste best chilled.

Nutritional Content of One Serving:
Calories: 102 Fat: 8.6g Protein: 1.4g Carbohydrates: 5.5g

Chocolate Nutella Cookies

Total Time Taken: 1 ¼ hours
Yield: 30 Servings
Ingredients:

- ¼ cup cocoa powder
- ¼ cup white sugar
- ½ teaspoon baking soda
- ½ teaspoon salt
- ¾ cup light brown sugar
- 1 cup butter, softened
- 1 cup dark chocolate chips
- 1 cup Nutella
- 1 teaspoon vanilla extract
- 2 cups all-purpose flour
- 2 eggs

Directions:

1. Mix the butter and sugars in a container until creamy and fluffy.
2. Put in the Nutella, vanilla and eggs and mix thoroughly.
3. Fold in the remaining ingredients then drop spoonfuls of batter on a baking tray covered with parchment paper.
4. Preheat your oven and bake the cookies at 350F for about fifteen minutes or until a golden-brown colour is achieved.
5. Serve the cookie chilled.

Nutritional Content of One Serving:
Calories: 136 Fat: 8.0g Protein: 1.8g Carbohydrates: 15.5g

Chocolate Orange Shortbread Cookies

Total Time Taken: 1 hour
Yield: 20 Servings
Ingredients:

- ¼ cup cocoa powder
- ¼ teaspoon salt
- ½ cup almond flour
- ½ cup butter, softened
- ½ cup white sugar

- ½ teaspoon baking soda
- 1 ½ cups all-purpose flour
- 1 egg
- 1 tablespoon orange zest
- 1 teaspoon vanilla extract

Directions:

1. Mix the butter, cocoa powder and sugar in a container until fluffy and pale.
2. Put in the egg, vanilla and orange zest and mix thoroughly.
3. Fold in the flour, almond flour, salt and baking soda then transfer the dough on a floured working surface.
4. Roll the dough into a slim sheet then cut small cookies using a cookie cutter of your choice.
5. Preheat your oven and bake the cookies at 350F for about fifteen minutes or until a golden-brown colour is achieved and fragrant.
6. These cookies taste best chilled.

Nutritional Content of One Serving:

Calories: 104 Fat: 5.4g Protein: 1.6g Carbohydrates: 13.0g

Chocolate Pecan Cookies

Total Time Taken: 1 hour
Yield: 10 Servings
Ingredients:

- ¼ teaspoon salt
- ½ cup dark chocolate chips
- 1 cup ground pecans
- 1 teaspoon vanilla extract
- 2 egg whites
- 2/3 cup white sugar

Directions:

1. Whip the egg whites and salt in a container until fluffy and airy.
2. Put in the sugar, progressively, and stir until shiny.
3. Fold in the pecans and chocolate chips then drop spoonfuls of batter on a baking sheet coated with baking paper.
4. Preheat your oven and bake the cookies at 350F for about fifteen minutes or until a z
5. These cookies taste best chilled.

Nutritional Content of One Serving:

Calories: 92 Fat: 2.6g Protein: 1.3g Carbohydrates: 17.6g

Chocolate Sandwich Cookies With Passionfruit Ganache

Total Time Taken: 2 hours
Yield: 30 Servings
Ingredients:
Cookies:

- ½ cup cocoa powder
- ½ teaspoon salt
- 1 cup white sugar
- 1 egg
- 1 teaspoon baking powder
- 1 teaspoon vanilla extract
- 2 cups all-purpose flour
- 2/3 cup butter, softened

Passionfruit Ganache:

- ¼ cup passionfruit juice
- ½ cup heavy cream
- 1 cup white chocolate chips
- 2 tablespoons butter

Directions:

1. For the cookies, combine the flour, cocoa powder, baking powder and salt in a container.
1. In a separate container, combine the butter and sugar until fluffy and pale.
2. Stir in the egg and vanilla and mix thoroughly then fold in the flour.
3. Transfer the dough to a floured working surface and roll it into a slim sheet.
4. Cut 40 small cookies using a round cookie cutter and arrange them on a baking sheet coated with baking paper.
5. For the ganache, bring the cream to a boil. Stir in the chocolate and stir until it melts completely. Put in the passionfruit juice and butter and mix thoroughly. Let cool in your refrigerator.
6. Fill the cookies with chilled ganache.

Nutritional Content of One Serving:
Calories: 143 Fat: 7.8g Protein: 1.7g Carbohydrates: 17.6g

Chocolate Star Anise Cookies

Total Time Taken: 1 ¼ hours
Yield: 20 Servings
Ingredients:

- ½ cup butter, softened
- ½ cup cocoa powder
- ½ cup pecans, chopped
- ½ teaspoon baking soda

- ½ teaspoon salt
- ¾ cup white sugar
- 1 ½ cups all-purpose flour
- 1 egg
- 1 teaspoon ground star anise
- 2 tablespoons coconut oil

Directions:

1. Mix the butter and coconut oil in a container. Put in the sugar and stir until fluffy.
2. Stir in the egg and stir thoroughly until blended.
3. Fold in the remaining ingredients and mix using a spatula.
4. Drop spoonfuls of batter on baking trays covered with parchment paper.
5. Pre-heat the oven and bake at 350F for about fifteen minutes or until risen and fragrant.
6. These cookies taste best chilled.

Nutritional Content of One Serving:

Calories: 129 Fat: 7.1g Protein: 1.8g Carbohydrates: 16.1g

Chunky Peanut Butter Cookies

Total Time Taken: 1 ¼ hours
Yield: 30 Servings

Ingredients:

- ¼ teaspoon salt
- ½ cup butter, softened
- 1 cup light brown sugar
- 1 cup peanut butter, softened
- 1 cup peanuts, chopped
- 1 egg
- 1 teaspoon baking powder
- 2 cups all-purpose flour

Directions:

1. Mix the butter and peanut butter in a container until creamy. Put in the sugar and mix for five minutes until fluffy.
2. Put in the egg and mix thoroughly then fold in the remaining ingredients.
3. Drop spoonfuls of batter on a baking tray coated with baking paper.
4. Preheat your oven and bake the cookies at 350F for about fifteen minutes or until a golden-brown colour is achieved on the edges.
5. Allow the cookies cool down before you serve.

Nutritional Content of One Serving:

Calories: 156 Fat: 10.0g Protein: 4.5g Carbohydrates: 13.7g

Raisin Bran Muffins

Total Time Taken: 1 hour
Yield: 10 Servings
Ingredients:

- ¼ teaspoon ground ginger
- ½ cup canola oil
- ½ cup golden raisins
- ½ cup white sugar
- ½ cup whole milk
- ½ teaspoon cinnamon powder
- ½ teaspoon salt
- 1 cup all-purpose flour
- 1 cup wheat bran
- 2 eggs
- 2 teaspoons baking powder

Directions:

1. Mix the flour, wheat bran, baking powder, salt, cinnamon, ginger and raisins in a container.
2. Put in the sugar, canola oil and eggs, as well as milk and mix using a spatula.
3. Spoon the batter in a muffin tin covered with muffin papers.
4. Preheat your oven and bake the muffins at 350F for about twenty minutes or until it rises significantly and starts to appear golden-brown.
5. *These muffins taste best cold.*

Nutritional Content of One Serving:

Calories: 235 Fat: 12.6g Protein: 3.9g Carbohydrates: 30.1g

Raspberry Jam Muffins

Total Time Taken: 1 hour
Yield: 12 Servings
Ingredients:

- 2 eggs
- 1 teaspoon vanilla extract
- ½ cup canola oil
- ¾ cup sour cream
- 1 ¾ cups all-purpose flour
- ½ teaspoon salt
- 1 ½ teaspoons baking powder
- 1 cup raspberry jam
- 2/3 cup white sugar

Directions:

1. Mix the eggs and sugar in a container until fluffy and pale, minimum volume increases to twice what it was.
2. Stir in the vanilla, sour cream and oil and mix thoroughly.
3. Fold in the flour, salt and baking powder then spoon the batter in a muffin tin coated with baking muffin papers.
4. Spoon the jam over each muffin and preheat your oven and bake at 350F for about twenty minutes or until a golden-brown colour is achieved and it rises significantly.
5. *Let cool down before you serve.*

Nutritional Content of One Serving:
Calories: 298 Fat: 13.0g Protein: 3.4g Carbohydrates: 43.4g

Raspberry Muffins

Total Time Taken: 1 hour
Yield: 10 Servings
Ingredients:

- ½ cup milk
- ½ cup white sugar
- ½ teaspoon salt
- 1 ½ teaspoons baking powder
- 1 cup fresh raspberries
- 1 teaspoon vanilla extract
- 2 cups all-purpose flour
- 3 eggs

Directions:

1. Mix the flour, sugar, salt and baking powder in a container.
2. Put in the remaining ingredients and mix using a spatula.
3. Spoon the batter in a muffin tin covered with muffin papers.
4. Preheat your oven and bake the muffins at 350F for about twenty minutes or until a toothpick inserted into the center of a muffin comes out clean.

These muffins taste best chilled.

Nutritional Content of One Serving:
Calories: 162 Fat: 1.9g Protein: 4.8g Carbohydrates: 31.7g

Raspberry Ricotta Muffins

Total Time Taken: 1 hour
Yield: 12 Servings
Ingredients:

- 2 eggs
- 1/3 cup white sugar
- 1/3 cup butter, softened
- 1 teaspoon vanilla extract
- 1 cup raspberries

- 1 ¾ cups all-purpose flour
- 1 ½ teaspoons baking powder
- ¾ cup ricotta cheese
- ½ cup milk
- ¼ teaspoon salt

Directions:

1. Mix the butter, cheese, sugar, eggs, milk and vanilla in a container.
2. Put in the flour, salt and baking powder then spoon the batter in a muffin tin covered with muffin papers.
3. Top each muffin with fresh raspberries and preheat your oven and bake at 350F for about twenty minutes or until it rises significantly and starts to appear golden-brown.

These muffins taste best chilled.

Nutritional Content of One Serving:

Calories: 176 Fat: 7.5g Protein: 5.1g Carbohydrates: 22.4g

Raspberry Vanilla Cupcakes

Total Time Taken: 1 ½ hours
Yield: 12 Servings
Ingredients:

Cupcakes:

- ½ cup butter, softened
- 2 eggs
- 1 tablespoon vanilla extract
- 1 ½ cups all-purpose flour
- ¼ teaspoon salt
- 1 ½ teaspoons baking powder
- 2/3 cup white sugar
- 2/3 cup buttermilk

Frosting:

- 1 cup fresh raspberries
- 1 teaspoon vanilla extract
- 2 cups heavy cream
- 2 tablespoons powdered sugar

Directions:

1. To make the cupcakes, combine the butter and sugar until pale and light.
2. Put in the eggs, one at a time, then mix in the vanilla and buttermilk.
3. Fold in the flour, salt and baking powder then spoon the batter in a muffin tin covered with muffin papers.
4. Preheat your oven and bake the cupcakes at 350F for about twenty minutes until a toothpick inserted into them comes out dry then allow them to cool down.

5. To make the frosting, whip the cream in a container until airy and puffed up. Put in the sugar and vanilla and mix thoroughly.
6. Drop a dollop of cream over each cupcake and garnish with a few raspberries.

Nutritional Content of One Serving:
Calories: 267 Fat: 16.1g Protein: 3.6g Carbohydrates: 27.3g

Raspberry White Chocolate Muffins

Total Time Taken: 1 hour
Yield: 12 Servings
Ingredients:

- ½ cup sour cream
- ½ cup white chocolate chips
- ½ cup white sugar
- ½ teaspoon salt
- 1 ½ cups all-purpose flour
- 1 cup fresh raspberries
- 1 teaspoon baking powder
- 1 teaspoon vanilla extract
- 2 eggs

Directions:

1. Mix the eggs, sugar and vanilla in a container until fluffy and creamy.
2. Put in the sour cream and mix thoroughly then fold in the dry ingredients.
3. Stir in using a spatula the raspberries and white chocolate.
4. Spoon the batter in a muffin tin covered with muffin papers and preheat your oven and bake at 350F for about twenty minutes or until a golden-brown colour is achieved and it rises significantly.
5. Let the muffins cool to room temperature before you serve.

Nutritional Content of One Serving:
Calories: 164 Fat: 5.2g Protein: 3.4g Carbohydrates: 26.4g

Red Berries Cream Cheese Muffins

Total Time Taken: 1 hour
Yield: 12 Servings
Ingredients:

- ¼ teaspoon salt
- ½ cup butter, softened
- ½ cup heavy cream
- ½ cup sliced almonds
- ¾ cup white sugar
- 1 ½ cups all-purpose flour
- 1 cup cream cheese
- 1 cup mixed berries

- 1 teaspoon vanilla extract
- 2 eggs
- 2 teaspoons baking powder

Directions:

1. Mix the cream cheese and butter in a container.
2. Put in the sugar and eggs and mix thoroughly. Stir in the cream and vanilla and stir thoroughly until blended.
3. Fold in the flour, salt and baking powder then put in the berries.
4. Spoon the batter in a muffin tin covered with muffin papers.
5. Top the muffins with sliced almonds and preheat your oven and bake at 350F for about twenty minutes or until it rises significantly and starts to appear golden-brown.
6. *Let cool down before you serve.*

Nutritional Content of One Serving:

Calories: 298 Fat: 19.2g Protein: 5.1g Carbohydrates: 27.9g

Red Velvet Cupcakes

Total Time Taken: 1 ½ hours
Yield: 12 Servings
Ingredients:

Cupcakes:

- ½ cup buttermilk
- ½ teaspoon baking soda
- ½ teaspoon salt
- ½ teaspoon white wine vinegar
- ¾ cup canola oil
- ¾ cup white sugar
- 1 ½ cups all-purpose flour
- 1 egg
- 1 tablespoon cocoa powder
- 1 teaspoon baking powder
- 1 teaspoon red food coloring
- 1 teaspoon vanilla extract

Frosting:

- ½ cup butter, softened
- 1 cup cream cheese, softened
- 1 teaspoon vanilla extract
- 3 cups powdered sugar

Directions:

1. To make the cupcakes, sift the flour, baking soda, baking powder and cocoa powder in a container.
2. In a separate container, combine the oil, egg and sugar until creamy and pale.
3. Stir in the buttermilk, red food coloring, vinegar and vanilla extract.

4. Spoon the batter in a muffin tin covered with muffin papers.

5. Preheat your oven and bake the cupcakes at 350F for about twenty minutes or until well risen.

6. Let the cupcakes cool in the pan.

7. To make the frosting, combine the cream cheese and butter in a container. Put in the vanilla and mix thoroughly then mix in the sugar and continue mixing for five minutes until fluffy and airy.

8. Spoon the frosting in a pastry bag and top the cupcakes with it.

These cupcakes taste best when fresh.

Nutritional Content of One Serving:
Calories: 489 Fat: 28.7g Protein: 4.0g Carbohydrates: 55.9g

Red Wine Fig Cupcakes

Total Time Taken: 1 ½ hours
Yield: 16 Servings
Ingredients:

Cupcakes:
- ½ cup red wine
- 1 teaspoon vanilla extract
- 2 eggs
- 1 ½ cups all-purpose flour
- ¼ cup cocoa powder
- ¼ teaspoon salt
- 1 ½ teaspoons baking powder
- 2/3 cup butter, softened
- 2/3 cup white sugar

Frosting:
- ½ cup butter, softened
- 1 cup cream cheese
- 2 cups powdered sugar

Fig compote:
- ¼ cup light brown sugar
- ½ cup red wine
- 1 cinnamon stick
- 6 figs, halved

Directions:
1. To make the cupcakes, combine the butter and sugar in a container until creamy. Put in the wine, vanilla and eggs and mix thoroughly.

2. Fold in the flour, cocoa powder, salt and baking powder and mix using a spatula.

3. Spoon the batter in a muffin tin covered with muffin papers.

4. Pre-heat the oven and bake at 350F for about twenty minutes or until it rises significantly and seems golden.

5. Let the muffins cool to room temperature in the pan.

6. To make the frosting, combine the butter and cream cheese in a container until fluffy and pale.
7. Put in the sugar, ½ cup at a time and stir thoroughly for 4-5 minutes until airy.
8. Pipe the frosting over each cupcake.
9. For the compote, mix the ingredients in a saucepan and cook for about five minutes just until softened.
    10. Top rach cupcake with the compote and serve fresh.

Nutritional Content of One Serving:
Calories: 353 Fat: 19.4g Protein: 3.6g Carbohydrates: 40.9g

Rhubarb Strawberry Muffins

Total Time Taken: 1 hour
Yield: 12 Servings
Ingredients:

- ½ cup light brown sugar
- ½ cup milk
- ½ cup whole wheat flour
- ½ teaspoon salt
- 1 cup all-purpose flour
- 1 cup strawberries, sliced
- 1 rhubarb stalk, sliced
- 1 teaspoon baking soda
- 1 teaspoon vanilla extract
- 3 eggs

Directions:

1. Mix the flours, salt and baking soda in a container.
2. Whip the eggs and sugar in a container until pale and light.
3. Put in the milk and vanilla and mix thoroughly.
4. Fold in the flour mixture then put in the rhubarb and strawberries.
5. Spoon the batter in a muffin tin covered with muffin papers.
6. Preheat your oven and bake the muffins at 350F for about twenty minutes or until a golden-brown colour is achieved and fluffy.

These muffins taste best chilled.

Nutritional Content of One Serving:
Calories: 106 Fat: 1.5g Protein: 3.5g Carbohydrates: 19.6g

Rhubarb Streusel Muffins

Total Time Taken: 1 ¼ hours
Yield: 12 Servings
Ingredients: **Muffins:**

- 2 rhubarb stalks, sliced
- 2 eggs
- 2 cups all-purpose flour

- 1 teaspoon baking powder
- 1 cup buttermilk
- ½ teaspoon baking soda
- ½ cup light brown sugar
- ¼ teaspoon salt
- ¼ cup white sugar
- ¼ cup canola oil

Streusel:
- 2 tablespoons white sugar
- 1 pinch salt
- 1 cup all-purpose flour
- ½ cup butter, melted

Directions:
1. For the muffins, combine the flour, baking soda, baking powder, salt and sugars in a container.
2. Put in the eggs, buttermilk and oil and mix using a spatula.
3. Fold in the rhubarb then spoon the batter in a muffin tin coated with baking muffin papers.
4. For the streusel, combine the ingredients in a container until grainy. Spread the
5. streusel over each muffin.
6. Pre-heat the oven and bake at 350F for about twenty minutes or until a golden-brown colour is achieved and it rises significantly.

These muffins taste best chilled.

Nutritional Content of One Serving:
Calories: 289 Fat: 13.4g Protein: 5.0g Carbohydrates: 37.6g

Rich Chocolate Muffins

Total Time Taken: 1 hour
Yield: 12 Servings
Ingredients:
- ¼ teaspoon baking soda
- ½ cup canola oil
- ½ cup cocoa powder
- ½ teaspoon salt
- ¾ cup milk
- 1 ¾ cups all-purpose flour
- 1 cup white sugar
- 1 teaspoon baking powder
- 1 teaspoon vanilla extract
- 2 eggs

Directions:
1. Mix the flour, cocoa powder, salt, baking powder, baking soda and salt in a container.
2. Put in the remaining ingredients and mix thoroughly.

3. Pour the batter in a muffin tin covered with muffin papers.
4. Preheat your oven and bake the muffins at 350F for about twenty minutes.
5. Let them cool in the pan before you serve or storing.

Nutritional Content of One Serving:
Calories: 237 Fat: 10.8g Protein: 3.9g Carbohydrates: 33.6g

Ricotta Lemon Muffins

Total Time Taken: 1 hour
Yield: 12 Servings
Ingredients:

- ¼ cup butter, melted
- ½ cup white sugar
- ½ teaspoon salt
- 1 ½ cups all-purpose flour
- 1 cup ricotta cheese
- 1 tablespoon lemon zest
- 1 teaspoon baking powder
- 1 teaspoon vanilla extract
- 2 eggs

Directions:

1. Mix the cheese, butter, eggs, vanilla and sugar in a container.
2. Put in the flour, salt and baking powder and mix using a spatula.
3. Spoon the batter in a muffin tin covered with muffin papers.
4. Preheat your oven and bake the muffins at 350F for about twenty minutes or until a golden-brown colour is achieved and it rises significantly.

These muffins taste best chilled.

Nutritional Content of One Serving:
Calories: 163 Fat: 6.3g Protein: 4.9g Carbohydrates: 21.7g

S'mores Chocolate Cupcakes

Total Time Taken: 1 ½ hours
Yield: 12 Servings
Ingredients:
Cupcakes:

- ¼ cup cocoa powder
- ¼ teaspoon salt
- ½ cup butter, softened
- ½ cup buttermilk
- ½ cup white sugar
- ½ teaspoon baking soda
- 1 ½ cups all-purpose flour

- 1 teaspoon baking powder
- 1 teaspoon vanilla extract
- 2 eggs
- 2 tablespoons dark brown sugar

Frosting:
- ½ cup crushed graham crackers
- ½ cup dark chocolate chips
- ½ cup white sugar
- 1 teaspoon vanilla extract
- 2 egg whites

Directions:

1. To make the cupcakes, combine the flour, cocoa powder, baking soda, baking powder and salt in a container.
2. Mix the butter and sugars in a separate container until creamy and pale.
3. Put in the eggs, buttermilk and vanilla and mix thoroughly.
4. Fold in the flour mixture then spoon the batter in a muffin tin coated with baking muffin papers.
5. Pre-heat the oven and bake at 350F for about twenty minutes or until it is aromatic and appears golden brown.
6. Let cool in the pan.
7. To make the frosting, combine the egg whites, sugar and vanilla in a container and place over a hot water bath. Keep on heat until the sugar is melted.
8. Turn off the heat and whip using an electric mixer until fluffy, stiff and shiny.
9. Apply the frosting on top of each cupcake and drizzle with chocolate chips and graham crackers.

These cupcakes taste best when fresh.

Nutritional Content of One Serving:

Calories: 255 Fat: 10.6g Protein: 4.4g Carbohydrates: 37.9g

Simple Lavender Cupcakes

Total Time Taken: 1 ½ hours
Yield: 12 Servings
Ingredients:

Cupcakes:
- ½ cup butter, softened
- 2 eggs
- 1 teaspoon vanilla extract
- 1 teaspoon lavender buds
- ½ cup heavy cream
- 1 ½ cups all-purpose flour
- ½ teaspoon salt
- 1 teaspoon baking powder
- 2/3 cup white sugar

Frosting:

- ¾ cup butter, softened
- 1 cup cream cheese
- 2 ½ cups powdered sugar

Directions:

1. To make the cupcakes, combine the butter and sugar in a container until creamy and pale.
2. Put in the eggs and vanilla and mix thoroughly. Stir in the lavender buds and cream and mix thoroughly.
3. Fold in the flour, salt and baking powder then spoon the batter in a muffin tin coated with baking muffin papers.
4. Pre-heat the oven and bake at 350F for about twenty minutes or until it rises significantly and starts to appear golden-brown.
5. Let them cool in the pan.
6. To make the frosting, combine the cream cheese and butter in a container until fluffy.
7. Put in the sugar and stir thoroughly for five minutes on high speed.
8. Top each cupcake with the frosting and serve them fresh.

Nutritional Content of One Serving:

Calories: 466 Fat: 28.8g Protein: 4.4g Carbohydrates: 49.8g

Snickerdoodle Muffins

Total Time Taken: 1 hour
Yield: 12 Servings
Ingredients:

Muffins:

- ½ cup butter, softened
- ½ cup light brown sugar
- ½ teaspoon ground ginger
- ½ teaspoon salt
- 1 teaspoon vanilla extract
- 2 ¼ cups all-purpose flour
- 2 eggs
- 2 teaspoons baking powder
- 2/3 cup buttermilk

Topping:

- 1 teaspoon cinnamon powder
- 2/3 cup white sugar

Directions:

1. For the muffins, combine the butter and sugar in a container.
2. Put in the vanilla and eggs and mix thoroughly then mix in the buttermilk.
3. Fold in the flour, salt, baking powder and ginger then spoon the batter in a muffin tin covered with muffin papers.

4. Pre-heat the oven and bake at 350F for about twenty minutes or until a golden-brown colour is achieved and it rises significantly.

5. For the topping, combine the ingredients in a container.

6. While the muffins are still hot, immerse them in cinnamon sugar.

These muffins taste best chilled.

Nutritional Content of One Serving:

Calories: 236 Fat: 8.8g Protein: 3.9g Carbohydrates: 36.1g

Snickers Cupcakes

Total Time Taken: 1 ½ hours
Yield: 16 Servings
Ingredients:

Cupcakes:

- ¼ teaspoon salt
- ½ cup canola oil
- ½ cup cocoa powder
- 1 ½ cups all-purpose flour
- 1 ½ teaspoons baking powder
- 1 cup buttermilk
- 1 cup light brown sugar
- 1 teaspoon lemon juice
- 1 teaspoon vanilla extract
- 4 eggs

Frosting:

- ½ cup butter, softened
- ½ cup cocoa powder
- ½ cup smooth peanut butter
- 1 teaspoon vanilla extract
- 2 cups powdered sugar

Topping:

- 6 snickers, chopped

Directions:

1. To make the cupcakes, combine the eggs and sugar in a container until fluffy and pale. Put in the oil and mix thoroughly then mix in the buttermilk, lemon juice and vanilla.

2. Fold in the flour, cocoa powder, salt and baking powder then spoon the batter in a muffin tin covered with muffin papers.

3. Preheat your oven and bake the cupcakes at 350F for about twenty minutes or until a toothpick inserted into them comes out dry.

4. Let cool down in the pan.

5. To make the frosting, combine the butter and peanut butter in a container until fluffy.

6. Stir in the sugar, cocoa powder and vanilla and stir thoroughly for a few additional minutes until fluffy and well mixed.

145

7. Pipe the frosting over each cupcake and serve them fresh.

Nutritional Content of One Serving:

Calories: 399 Fat: 22.4g Protein: 7.4g Carbohydrates: 45.8g

Sour Cream Muffins

Total Time Taken: 1 hour
Yield: 12 Servings
Ingredients:

- ¼ teaspoon salt
- 1 ½ cups sour cream
- 1 cup butter, softened
- 1 teaspoon vanilla extract
- 2 cups all-purpose flour
- 2 teaspoons baking powder

Directions:

1. Mix the butter, vanilla and sour cream in a container until creamy.
2. Put in the flour, salt and baking powder then spoon the batter in a muffin tin coated with baking muffin papers.
3. Pre-heat the oven and bake at 350F for about twenty minutes or until it rises significantly and starts to appear golden-brown.

These muffins taste best chilled.

Nutritional Content of One Serving:

Calories: 275 Fat: 21.6g Protein: 3.2g Carbohydrates: 17.6g

Spelt Zucchini Muffins

Total Time Taken: 1 ¼ hours
Yield: 12 Servings
Ingredients:

- ¼ cup coconut oil, melted
- ¼ cup maple syrup
- ¼ teaspoon salt
- ½ cup plain yogurt
- 1 cup grated zucchinis
- 1 cup spelt flour
- 1 cup whole wheat flour
- 1 egg
- 1 teaspoon baking soda
- 1 teaspoon vanilla extract
- 2 tablespoons chia seeds

Directions:

1. Mix the spelt flour, wheat flour, salt and baking soda in a container.

2. Put in the remaining ingredients and stir for a few seconds to mix.

3. Spoon the batter in a muffin tin covered with muffin papers and preheat your oven and bake at 350F for about twenty minutes or until a toothpick inserted in the center comes out clean.

4. *Let cool down before you serve.*

Nutritional Content of One Serving:

Calories: 169 Fat: 6.9g Protein: 4.7g Carbohydrates: 22.5g

Coffee Gingersnap Cookies

Total Time Taken: 1 ¼ hours
Yield: 20 Servings
Ingredients:

- ¼ cup coconut oil
- ¼ teaspoon salt
- ½ cup butter, softened
- ½ teaspoon ground cardamom
- 1 cup light brown sugar
- 1 egg
- 1 teaspoon baking soda
- 1 teaspoon cinnamon powder
- 1 teaspoon ground ginger
- 1 teaspoon vanilla extract
- 2 cups all-purpose flour
- 2 teaspoons instant coffee

Directions:

1. Mix the butter, coconut oil and brown sugar in a container until fluffy and creamy.

2. Put in the egg and vanilla and mix thoroughly.

3. Fold in the remaining ingredients then drop spoonfuls of batter on a baking sheet coated with baking paper.

4. Pre-heat the oven and bake at 350F for fifteen minutes or until aromatic and crunchy.

5. These cookies taste best chilled.

Nutritional Content of One Serving:

Calories: 142 Fat: 7.7g Protein: 1.7g Carbohydrates: 16.8g

Coffee Shortbread Cookies

Total Time Taken: 1 hour
Yield: 20 Servings
Ingredients:

- ½ cup butter, softened
- ½ cup powdered sugar
- ½ teaspoon baking powder
- ½ teaspoon salt

- 1 egg
- 1 teaspoon vanilla extract
- 2 cups all-purpose flour
- 2 teaspoons instant coffee

Directions:

1. Mix the butter, sugar and vanilla and stir until smooth and fluffy.
2. Put in the egg and mix thoroughly then fold in the flour, salt, baking powder and coffee.
3. Put the dough on a floured working surface and roll it into a slim sheet.
4. Cut into small cookies using a cookie cutter of your choices and position the cookies on a baking sheet coated with baking paper.
5. Preheat your oven and bake the cookies at 350F for about fifteen minutes or until it is aromatic and appears golden-brown on the edges.
6. Serve Chilled or store them in an airtight container.

Nutritional Content of One Serving:

Calories: 102 Fat: 5.0g Protein: 1.6g Carbohydrates: 12.6g

Colorful Chocolate Cookies

Total Time Taken: 1 ¼ hors
Yield: 30 Servings

Ingredients:

- ½ cup cocoa powder
- ½ cup crushed candy cane cookies
- ½ cup M&M candies
- ½ teaspoon salt
- 1 cup butter, softened
- 1 cup light brown sugar
- 1 egg
- 1 teaspoon baking powder
- 1 teaspoon vanilla extract
- 2 cups all-purpose flour

Directions:

1. Mix the butter, sugar and vanilla and stir thoroughly until fluffy and pale.
2. Stir in the egg and mix thoroughly then put in the remaining ingredients.
3. Drop spoonfuls of batter on a baking tray coated with baking paper.
4. Pre-heat the oven and bake at 350F for about fifteen minutes.
5. Let the cookies cool in the pan before you serve.

Nutritional Content of One Serving:

Calories: 129 Fat: 7.4g Protein: 1.5g Carbohydrates: 14.8g

Confetti Cookies

Total Time Taken: 1 ¼ hours
 Yield: 20 Servings
Ingredients:

- 1 teaspoon vanilla extract
- 1 egg
- 2 cups all-purpose flour
- 1 teaspoon baking powder
- ¼ teaspoon salt
- ½ cup colourful sprinkles
- 2/3 cup butter, softened
- 2/3 cup white sugar

Directions:

1. Mix the butter with sugar and vanilla in a container until creamy and fluffy.
2. Stir in the egg and mix thoroughly then fold in the remaining ingredients.
3. Drop in the sprinkles and mix using a spatula.
4. Drop spoonfuls of batter on a baking sheet coated with baking paper.
5. Pre-heat the oven and bake at 350F for about fifteen minutes or until a golden-brown colour is achieved on the edges.
6. These cookies taste best chilled.

Nutritional Content of One Serving:

Calories: 136 Fat: 6.7g Protein: 1.7g Carbohydrates: 17.5g

Cornflake Chocolate Chip Cookies

Total Time Taken: 1 hour
 Yield: 20 Servings
Ingredients:

- ½ cup butter, softened
- ½ cup dark chocolate chips
- ½ teaspoon baking soda
- ¾ cup white sugar
- 1 ¼ cup all-purpose flour
- 1 cup cornflakes
- 1 egg
- 1 teaspoon vanilla extract
- 2/4 teaspoon salt

Directions:

1. Mix the butter, sugar and vanilla in a container until creamy and pale.
2. Put in the egg then mix in the flour, baking soda and salt.
3. Fold in the cornflakes and chocolate chips.

4. Drop spoonfuls of batter on a baking sheet coated with baking paper.

5. Preheat your oven and bake the cookies at 350F for about fifteen minutes or until a golden-brown colour is achieved on the edges.

6. *These cookies taste best chilled.*

Nutritional Content of One Serving:

Calories: 120 Fat: 5.7g Protein: 1.4g Carbohydrates: 16.7g

Cracked Sugar Cookies

Total Time Taken: 1 ¼ hours
Yield: 30 Servings

Ingredients:

- ½ teaspoon salt
- 1 cup butter, softened
- 1 cup powdered sugar
- 1 cup white sugar
- 1 teaspoon baking soda
- 1 teaspoon vanilla extract
- 2 ½ cups all-purpose flour
- 3 egg yolks

Directions:

1. Mix the butter and sugar in a container until creamy and fluffy.
2. Put in the egg yolks and mix thoroughly then mix in the vanilla.
3. Fold in the flour, baking soda and salt then form small balls of dough and roll them through powdered sugar.
4. Put the balls on a baking tray coated with baking paper.
5. Pre-heat the oven and bake at 350F for about fifteen minutes or until mildly golden brown.
6. These cookies taste best chilled, handling them with care.

Nutritional Content of One Serving:

Calories: 139 Fat: 6.7g Protein: 1.4g Carbohydrates: 18.7g

Cranberry Biscotti

Total Time Taken: 1 ½ hours
Yield: 20 Servings

Ingredients:

- ¼ teaspoon salt
- ½ cup butter, softened
- ½ cup white sugar
- ½ teaspoon baking soda
- 1 cup dried cranberries
- 1 egg
- 1 tablespoon lemon zest

- 2 cups all-purpose flour

Directions:

1. Mix the butter and sugar in a container until creamy and fluffy.
2. Put in the egg and lemon zest and mix thoroughly.
3. Stir in the flour, baking soda and salt then put in the cranberries.
4. Put the dough on a baking tray coated with baking paper. Shape the dough into a log and bake it in the preheated oven at 350F for fifteen minutes.
5. Remove the tray from the oven and allow it to cool down for about ten minutes. Cut the log into 1cm wide slices and place them back on the tray with the cut facing up.
6. Carry on baking for fifteen minutes or until a golden-brown colour is achieved and crisp.
7. Let cool before you serve or storing.

Nutritional Content of One Serving:

Calories: 111 Fat: 5.0g Protein: 1.6g Carbohydrates: 15.1g

Custard Powder Cookies

Total Time Taken: 1 ¼ hours
Yield: 20 Servings

Ingredients:

- ¼ cup whole milk
- ¼ teaspoon salt
- ½ cup butter, softened
- ½ cup vanilla custard powder
- ½ cup white sugar
- 1 ½ cups all-purpose flour
- 1 teaspoon baking powder
- 1 teaspoon vanilla extract

Directions:

1. Mix the butter and sugar in a container until creamy and fluffy.
2. Stir in the milk and vanilla then fold in the remaining ingredients.
3. Drop spoonfuls of batter on a baking sheet coated with baking paper.
4. Preheat your oven and bake the cookies at 350F for about fifteen minutes or until a golden-brown colour is achieved on the edges.
5. *These cookies taste best chilled.*

Nutritional Content of One Serving:

Calories: 115 Fat: 4.8g Protein: 1.1g Carbohydrates: 17.3g

Date Pecan Ginger Cookies

Total Time Taken: 1 ½ hours
Yield: 30 Servings

Ingredients:

- ¼ teaspoon salt
- ½ cup olive oil

- ½ cup whole wheat flour
- 1 cup all-purpose flour
- 1 cup dates, pitted and chopped
- 1 cup light brown sugar
- 1 cup pecans, chopped
- 1 egg
- 1 teaspoon baking powder
- 1 teaspoon grated ginger
- 1 teaspoon vanilla extract

Directions:

1. Mix the oil and sugar in a container until fluffy and pale.
2. Put in the vanilla and ginger and mix thoroughly then fold in the flours, baking powder and salt.
3. Stir in the dates and pecans then drop spoonfuls of batter on a baking sheet coated with baking paper.
4. Preheat your oven and bake the cookies at 350F for fifteen minutes or until a golden-brown colour is achieved on the edges.
5. *These cookies taste best chilled.*

Nutritional Content of One Serving:

Calories: 93 Fat: 3.9g Protein: 1.0g Carbohydrates: 14.2g

Double Chocolate Cookies

Total Time Taken: 1 ½ hours
Yield: 30 Servings

Ingredients:

- ¼ teaspoon salt
- ½ cup cocoa powder
- ½ cup mini chocolate chips
- ½ teaspoon baking powder
- 1 ½ cups all-purpose flour
- 1 cup white sugar
- 1 egg
- 1 teaspoon vanilla extract
- 2/3 cup butter, softened

Directions:

1. Mix the butter and sugar until fluffy and creamy.
2. Put in the egg and vanilla and mix thoroughly then fold in the remaining ingredients and mix thoroughly.
3. Cover the dough with plastic wrap and store in the refrigerator for about half an hour.
4. Transfer the dough to a floured working surface and roll it into a slim sheet.
5. Cut into small cookies using a cookie cutter of your choices and place them on a baking pan coated with baking paper.
6. Pre-heat the oven and bake at 350F for about fifteen minutes.

7. *These cookies taste best chilled.*

Nutritional Content of One Serving:

Calories: 93 Fat: 4.6g Protein: 1.2g Carbohydrates: 12.8g

Double Chocolate Espresso Cookies

Total Time Taken: 1 hour
Yield: 20 Servings
Ingredients:

- 2 eggs
- 1 teaspoon vanilla extract
- ¼ cup coconut oil, melted
- 1 teaspoon instant coffee
- 6 oz. dark chocolate
- ¼ cup butter
- 2 tablespoons all-purpose flour
- ¼ teaspoon salt
- 2/3 cup white sugar

Directions:

1. Mix the chocolate and butter in a heatproof container and place over a hot water bath. Melt them together until smooth and melted.
2. Mix the eggs and sugar in a container until fluffy and pale. Put in the vanilla and oil and stir lightly. Stir in the coffee.
3. Put in the melted chocolate and stir lightly then fold in the flour and salt.
4. Drop spoonfuls of batter on a baking tray coated with baking paper.
5. Pre-heat the oven and bake at 350F for about ten minutes or until set.
6. *These cookies taste best chilled.*

Nutritional Content of One Serving:

Calories: 124 Fat: 8.0g Protein: 1.3g Carbohydrates: 12.4g

Double Ginger Cookies

Total Time Taken: 1 ¼ hours
Yield: 20 Servings
Ingredients:

- ¼ cup candied ginger, chopped
- ¼ teaspoon salt
- ½ teaspoon baking soda
- ½ teaspoon cinnamon powder
- 1 teaspoon ground ginger
- 1 teaspoon vanilla extract
- 1/3 cup butter, softened
- 2 cups all-purpose flour

- 2 tablespoons golden syrup
- 2/3 cup light brown sugar

Directions:

1. Sift the flour, ginger, cinnamon, salt and baking soda in a container.
2. Mix the butter, sugar, vanilla and syrup in a container until fluffy and pale.
3. Fold in the flour then put in the candied ginger.
4. Drop spoonfuls of batter on a baking sheet coated with baking paper.
5. Pre-heat the oven and bake at 350F for about fifteen minutes or until it rises and looks golden brown.
6. *These cookies taste best chilled.*

Nutritional Content of One Serving:

Calories: 98 Fat: 3.2g Protein: 1.4g Carbohydrates: 16.1g

Dried Cranberry Oatmeal Cookies

Total Time Taken: 1 ¼ hours
Yield: 20 Servings

Ingredients:

- ¼ teaspoon salt
- ½ cup butter, softened, melted
- ½ cup dried cranberries
- ½ cup light brown sugar
- ½ teaspoon cinnamon powder
- ½ teaspoon ground ginger
- 1 cup all-purpose flour
- 1 cup rolled oats
- 1 teaspoon baking soda
- 4 tablespoons golden syrup

Directions:

1. Mix the oats, flour, baking soda, spices, salt and cranberries in a container.
2. Stir in the butter, golden syrup and sugar and mix thoroughly.
3. Make small balls for dough and place the balls on a baking sheet coated with baking paper.
4. Flatten the cookies slightly and preheat your oven and bake at 350F for fifteen minutes or until a golden-brown colour is achieved and fragrant.
5. *These cookies taste best chilled.*

Nutritional Content of One Serving:

Calories: 106 Fat: 4.9g Protein: 1.2g Carbohydrates: 14.5g

Dried Fruit Wholesome Cookies

Total Time Taken: 1 ¼ hours
Yield: 20 Servings

Ingredients:

- ¼ cup applesauce

- ¼ cup coconut oil, melted
- ¼ cup dried apricots, chopped
- ¼ cup dried cranberries
- ¼ cup golden raisins
- ¼ cup rolled oats
- ¼ teaspoon salt
- ½ teaspoon baking soda
- ½ teaspoon cinnamon powder
- 1 ¼ cups whole wheat flour
- 1 egg
- 1 teaspoon vanilla extract

Directions:

1. Mix the coconut oil, applesauce, egg and vanilla and mix thoroughly.
2. Stir in the flour, salt, baking soda and cinnamon then put in the oats and dried fruits.
3. Drop spoonfuls of batter on a baking tray coated with baking paper.
4. Preheat your oven and bake the cookies at 350F for about ten minutes or until a golden-brown colour is achieved and crisp on the edges.
5. *These cookies taste best chilled.*

Nutritional Content of One Serving:

Calories: 68 Fat: 3.1g Protein: 1.3g Carbohydrates: 8.8g

Dried Prune Oatmeal Cookies

Total Time Taken: 1 ¼ hours
Yield: 25 Servings

Ingredients:

- ¼ teaspoon salt
- ½ cup coconut oil, melted
- ½ cup maple syrup
- ½ teaspoon baking soda
- ¾ cup all-purpose flour
- 1 cup dried prunes, chopped
- 1 teaspoon lemon juice
- 1 teaspoon vanilla extract
- 2 cups rolled oats

Directions:

1. Mix the prunes, oats, flour, baking soda and salt in a container.
2. Put in the rest of the ingredients and mix using a spatula.
3. Make small balls of dough and arrange them on a baking sheet coated with baking paper.
4. Preheat your oven and bake the cookies at 350F for about fifteen minutes or until a golden-brown colour is achieved.
5. *These cookies taste best chilled.*

Earl Grey Cookies

Total Time Taken: 1 ¼ hours
Yield: 20 Servings

Ingredients:

- ½ cup powdered sugar
- ½ teaspoon salt
- 1 cup butter, softened
- 1 egg
- 1 tablespoon loose Earl grey leaves
- 1 teaspoon baking powder
- 1 teaspoon vanilla extract
- 2 cups all-purpose flour

Directions:

1. Mix the butter and sugar in a container until fluffy and pale.
2. Put in the egg and vanilla and mix thoroughly.
3. Stir in the remaining ingredients and mix using a spatula.
4. Transfer the dough to a floured working surface and roll it into a slim sheet.
5. Cut into small cookies with your cookie cutters and place them on a baking tray coated with baking paper.
6. Pre-heat the oven and bake at 350F for about ten minutes or until a golden-brown colour is achieved on the edges.
7. *These cookies taste best chilled.*

Nutritional Content of One Serving:

Calories: 143 Fat: 9.6g Protein: 1.7g Carbohydrates: 12.7g

Eggless Cookies

Total Time Taken: 1 hour
Yield: 20 Servings

Ingredients:

- ¼ cup whole milk
- ¼ teaspoon salt
- ½ cup butter, melted
- ½ cup dried cranberries
- ½ cup light brown sugar
- ½ teaspoon baking soda
- 1 ½ cups all-purpose flour

Directions:

1. Mix the flour, salt, baking soda and sugar in a container.

2. Stir in the butter and milk and mix using a spatula.
3. Fold in the cranberries then drop spoonfuls of batter on a baking sheet coated with baking paper.
4. Pre-heat the oven and bake at 350F for about fifteen minutes or until a golden-brown colour is achieved on the edges.
5. *These cookies taste best chilled.*

Nutritional Content of One Serving:
Calories: 92 Fat: 4.8g Protein: 1.1g Carbohydrates: 11.1g

Fig and Almond Cookies

Total Time Taken: 1 ¼ hours
Yield: 20 Servings
Ingredients:

- ½ cup butter, softened
- ½ cup ground almonds
- ½ teaspoon baking soda
- ½ teaspoon salt
- 1 ½ cups dried figs, chopped
- 1 ¾ cups all-purpose flour
- 1 cup powdered sugar
- 1 egg
- 1 teaspoon vanilla extract

Directions:

1. Mix the butter, sugar and vanilla in a container until fluffy and pale.
2. Put in the egg and mix thoroughly then fold in the remaining ingredients.
3. Drop spoonfuls of batter on a baking tray coated with baking paper.
4. Pre-heat the oven and bake at 350F for about fifteen minutes or until a golden-brown colour is achieved on the edges and slightly crisp.
5. *These cookies taste best chilled.*

Nutritional Content of One Serving:
Calories: 159 Fat: 6.3g Protein: 2.5g Carbohydrates: 24.4g

Everything - But - The - Kitchen - Sink Cookies

Total Time Taken: 1 ¼ hours
Yield: 20 Servings
Ingredients:

- ¼ cup applesauce
- ¼ cup coconut oil, melted
- ¼ cup dark chocolate chips
- ¼ cup dried apricots, chopped

- ¼ cup dried cranberries
- ¼ cup shredded coconut
- ¼ teaspoon cinnamon powder
- ½ cup walnuts, chopped
- ½ teaspoon ground ginger
- ½ teaspoon salt
- 1 cup rolled oats
- 1 cup whole wheat flour
- 1 egg
- 1 teaspoon vanilla extract
- 2 tablespoons butter, softened

Directions:

1. Mix the coconut oil, butter, vanilla, egg and applesauce in a container.
2. Put in the flour, oats, spices and salt then fold in the walnuts, apricots, cranberries, apricots, chocolate chips and coconut.
3. Drop spoonfuls of batter on baking trays coated with baking paper.
4. Preheat your oven and bake the cookies at 350F for about fifteen minutes or until a golden-brown colour is achieved and crisp on the edges.
5. These cookies taste best chilled.

Nutritional Content of One Serving:

Calories: 109 Fat: 7.0g Protein: 2.4g Carbohydrates: 9.8g

Funfetti Banana Muffins

Total Time Taken: 1 hour
Yield: 12 Servings
Ingredients:

- ¼ cup colourful sprinkles
- ¼ teaspoon salt
- ½ cup almond flour
- ½ cup canola oil
- ½ cup milk
- ½ cup white sugar
- 1 ½ cups all-purpose flour
- 1 teaspoon baking powder
- 1 teaspoon vanilla extract
- 2 eggs

Directions:

1. Mix the eggs and sugar in a container until fluffy and pale.
2. Put in the oil, vanilla and milk and mix thoroughly.
3. Fold in the flours, salt and baking powder then put in the sprinkles.

4. Spoon the batter in a muffin tin covered with muffin papers and preheat your oven and bake at 350F for about twenty minutes or until a golden-brown colour is achieved and it rises significantly.

5. *Let cool down before you serve.*

Nutritional Content of One Serving:

Calories: 204 Fat: 11.2g Protein: 3.3g Carbohydrates: 23.3g

Funfetti Cream Cheese Cupcakes

Total Time Taken: 1 ½ hours
Yield: 12 Servings
Ingredients:

Cupcakes:

- ½ cup colourful sprinkles
- ½ cup butter, softened
- ½ cup milk
- ½ cup sour cream
- ½ teaspoon baking soda
- ½ teaspoon salt
- 1 ¾ cups all-purpose flour
- 1 teaspoon baking powder
- 1 teaspoon vanilla extract
- 2 eggs
- 2/3 cup white sugar

Frosting:

- ½ cup butter, softened
- 1 cup cream cheese
- 2 cups powdered sugar
- Sprinkles to garnish

Directions:

1. To make the cupcakes, combine the butter and sugar in a container until creamy and pale.
2. Put in the eggs and mix thoroughly then mix in the sour cream, milk and vanilla.
3. Fold in the sprinkles then spoon the batter in a muffin tin coated with baking muffin papers.
4. Pre-heat the oven and bake at 350F for about twenty minutes or until it rises significantly and starts to appear golden-brown.
5. Let the cupcakes cool down.
6. To make the frosting, combine the cream cheese and butter in a container until pale.
7. Put in the sugar and mix thoroughly for about five to seven minutes or until fluffy and light.
8. Garnish the cupcakes with cream cheese frosting.
9. *Top with colourful sprinkles.*

Nutritional Content of One Serving:

Calories: 438 Fat: 25.7g Protein: 5.2g Carbohydrates: 48.6g

German Chocolate Cupcakes

Total Time Taken: 1 ½ hours
Yield: Servings 18
Ingredients:

Cupcakes:

- 1 cup butter, softened
- ¼ cup light brown sugar
- 2 eggs
- 1 teaspoon vanilla extract
- 1 cup buttermilk
- ½ cup sour cream
- 1 cup cocoa powder
- ¼ teaspoon salt
- 1 ½ teaspoons baking powder
- ½ teaspoon baking soda
- 2/3 cup white sugar
- 1 3/4 cups all-purpose flour

Frosting:

- ½ cup pecans, chopped
- 1 cup butter, softened
- 1 cup evaporated milk
- 1 cup light brown sugar
- 1 cup sliced almonds
- 2 cups shredded coconut

Directions:

1. To make the cupcakes, combine the butter, sugars and vanilla in a container until fluffy and pale.
2. Put in the eggs, one at a time, and mix thoroughly then mix in the buttermilk and sour cream.
3. Fold in the flour, cocoa powder, salt, baking powder and baking soda.
4. Spoon the batter in a muffin tin covered with muffin papers.
5. Pre-heat the oven and bake at 350F for about twenty minutes.
6. To make the frosting, combine the butter, sugar and evaporated milk in a container until creamy and fluffy.
7. Put in the coconut, almonds and pecans and mix thoroughly.
8. Top each cupcake with the frosting and serve them fresh.

Nutritional Content of One Serving:

Calories: 415 Fat: 30.4g Protein: 6.1g Carbohydrates: 34.4g

Ginger Pineapple Muffins

Total Time Taken: 1 hour
Yield: 12 Servings
Ingredients:

- ½ cup canola oil
- ½ cup milk
- ½ cup shredded coconut
- ½ teaspoon cinnamon powder
- ½ teaspoon salt
- ¾ cup light brown sugar
- 1 ½ cups all-purpose flour
- 1 ½ teaspoons baking powder
- 1 cup crushed pineapple
- 1 egg
- 1 teaspoon ground ginger

Directions:

1. Mix the oil and sugar until creamy. Put in the egg and mix thoroughly then mix in the milk and mix very well.
2. Fold in the flour, coconut, salt, baking powder, ginger and cinnamon and mix thoroughly.
3. Fold in the pineapple then spoon the batter in a muffin tin covered with muffin papers.
4. Pre-heat the oven and bake at 350F for about twenty minutes or until it rises significantly and starts to appear golden-brown.

These muffins taste best chilled.

Nutritional Content of One Serving:
Calories: 202 Fat: 10.9g Protein: 2.6g Carbohydrates: 24.1g

Gingerbread Muffins

Total Time Taken: 1 hour
Yield: 12 Servings
Ingredients:

- ½ cup raisins
- ½ cup wheat bran
- ½ cup white sugar
- ½ teaspoon ground ginger
- ½ teaspoon ground star anise
- ½ teaspoon salt
- 1 ½ cups all-purpose flour
- 1 cup buttermilk
- 1 egg
- 1 teaspoon cinnamon powder

- 1 teaspoon vanilla extract
- 2 tablespoons dark molasses

Directions:
1. Mix the dry ingredients in a container.
2. Put in the wet ingredients and stir for a few seconds to mix.
3. Spoon the batter in a muffin tin covered with muffin papers.
4. Preheat your oven and bake the muffins at 350F for about twenty minutes or until it is aromatic and appears golden.
5. *Best served chilled.*

Nutritional Content of One Serving:
Calories: 137 Fat: 0.8g Protein: 3.4g Carbohydrates: 30.3g

Gluten Free Chocolate Cupcakes With Pumpkin Frosting

Total Time Taken: 1 ½ hours
Yield: 12 Servings
Ingredients:
Cupcakes:
- ¼ cup coconut oil, melted
- ¼ teaspoon salt
- ½ cup buckwheat flour
- ½ cup cocoa powder
- ½ cup coconut flour
- ½ cup maple syrup
- 1 cup shredded coconut
- 1 cup sparkling water
- 1 teaspoon baking soda
- 1 teaspoon vanilla extract

Frosting:
- ¼ teaspoon cinnamon powder
- ¼ teaspoon ground ginger
- ½ cup pumpkin puree
- ½ cup walnuts
- 1 cup dates, pitted
- 2 tablespoons coconut oil
- 2 tablespoons maple syrup

Directions:
1. To make the cupcakes, combine the flours, shredded coconut, cocoa powder, baking soda and salt in a container.

2. In a separate container, mix the maple syrup, sparkling water, coconut oil and vanilla and mix thoroughly. Put in the dry ingredients and stir for a few seconds to mix.

3. Pour the batter in a muffin tin covered with muffin papers and preheat your oven and bake at 350F for about twenty minutes or until a toothpick inserted into them comes out dry.

4. Let the cupcakes cool down.

5. To make the frosting, place the dates and the rest of the ingredients in a food processor or blender and pulse until well mixed.

6. Top each cupcake with the frosting and serve fresh.

Nutritional Content of One Serving:
Calories: 249 Fat: 13.5g Protein: 3.9g Carbohydrates: 32.8g

Gluten Free Chocolate Muffins

Total Time Taken: 1 hour
Yield: 10 Servings
Ingredients:

- ¼ cup cocoa powder
- ½ cup canola oil
- ½ cup dark chocolate chips
- ½ cup shredded coconut
- ½ cup tapioca flour
- ½ cup white rice flour
- ½ cup white sugar
- ½ teaspoon salt
- 1 teaspoon baking powder
- 1 teaspoon vanilla extract
- 3 eggs

Directions:

1. Mix the eggs, sugar and vanilla in a container until fluffy and pale.

2. Put in the oil then mix in the remaining ingredients.

3. Spoon the batter in a muffin tin covered with muffin papers and preheat your oven and bake at 350F for about twenty minutes or until it rises significantly and becomes aromatic.

These muffins taste best chilled.

Nutritional Content of One Serving:
Calories: 251 Fat: 15.4g Protein: 2.9g Carbohydrates: 28.7g

Gluten Free Maple Muffins

Total Time Taken: 1 hour
Yield: 12 Servings
Ingredients:

- ¼ cup tapioca flour
- ¼ teaspoon salt
- ½ cup butter, melted

- ½ cup coconut flour
- ½ cup maple syrup
- ½ cup sorghum flour
- ¾ cup milk
- 1 ½ teaspoons baking powder
- 1 teaspoon vanilla extract
- 2 eggs
- 2 tablespoons dark brown sugar

Directions:

1. Mix the eggs, butter, maple syrup, sugar and vanilla in a container until creamy.
2. Put in the remaining ingredients and mix thoroughly.
3. Pour the batter in a muffin tin covered with muffin papers.
4. Pre-heat the oven and bake at 350F for about twenty minutes or until a toothpick inserted into the center of a muffin comes out clean.
5. Let the muffins cool to room temperature before you serve.

Nutritional Content of One Serving:

Calories: 203 Fat: 9.7g Protein: 3.1g Carbohydrates: 27.3g

Grain Free Apple Cinnamon

Total Time Taken: 1 ¼ hours
Yield: 12 Servings

Ingredients:

- ¼ cup coconut oil, melted
- ¼ cup honey
- ¼ teaspoon salt
- ½ cup coconut milk
- ½ cup tapioca flour
- ½ teaspoon baking powder
- ½ teaspoon baking soda
- 1 ½ cups almond flour
- 1 teaspoon cinnamon powder
- 1 teaspoon lemon juice
- 1 teaspoon vanilla extract
- 2 red apples, cored and diced
- 3 eggs

Directions:

1. Mix the flours, cinnamon, baking soda, baking powder and salt in a container.
2. Put in the eggs and the remaining ingredients and mix thoroughly.
3. Spoon the batter in a muffin tin coated with baking muffin papers then preheat your oven and bake at 350F for about twenty minutes or until a golden-brown colour is achieved and it rises significantly.

These muffins taste best chilled.

Nutritional Content of One Serving:
Calories: 163 Fat: 9.8g Protein: 2.5g Carbohydrates: 18.5g

Grapefruit Cream Cheese Cupcakes

Total Time Taken: 1 ½ hours
Yield: 12 Servings
Ingredients:

Cupcakes:

- ½ cup butter, softened
- ½ teaspoon salt
- ¾ cup buttermilk
- ¾ cup white sugar
- 1 ½ teaspoons baking powder
- 1 ¾ cups all-purpose flour
- 1 teaspoon grapefruit zest
- 2 eggs

Frosting:

- ½ cup butter
- 1 cup cream cheese
- 1 tablespoon grapefruit zest
- 2 cups powder sugar

Directions:

1. To make the cupcakes, combine the butter and sugar in a container until fluffy and creamy.
2. Put in the zest and eggs and mix thoroughly.
3. Stir in the flour, salt and baking powder then put in the milk and mix thoroughly.
4. Spoon the batter in a muffin tin covered with muffin papers and preheat your oven and bake at 350F for about twenty minutes.
5. Let the cupcakes cool in the pan.
6. To make the frosting, combine the cream cheese and butter in a container until fluffy.
7. Put in the eggs and stir thoroughly for 4-5 minutes then mix in the zest.
8. Garnish each cupcake with frosting and serve them fresh.

Nutritional Content of One Serving:
Calories: 412 Fat: 23.1g Protein: 4.9g Carbohydrates: 48.1g

Harvest Muffins

Total Time Taken: 1 hour
Yield: 12 Servings
Ingredients:

- 2 eggs
- 2 cups all-purpose flour
- 1 teaspoon baking powder

- 1 pear, cored and diced
- 1 cup milk
- 1 apple, cored and diced
- ½ teaspoon ground ginger
- ½ teaspoon cinnamon powder
- ½ teaspoon baking soda
- ½ cup light brown sugar
- ½ cup dried cranberries
- ½ cup butter, melted
- ¼ teaspoon salt

Directions:

1. Mix the flour, baking powder, baking soda, salt, cinnamon, ginger and sugar in a container.
2. Put in the eggs, milk and butter and stir for a few seconds to mix.
3. Fold in the apple, pear and cranberries then spoon the batter in a muffin pan coated with muffin papers.
4. Pre-heat the oven and bake at 350F for about twenty minutes or until it rises significantly and becomes aromatic.
5. Let the muffins cool to room temperature before you serve.

Nutritional Content of One Serving:

Calories: 205 Fat: 9.1g Protein: 3.9g Carbohydrates: 27.4g

Hazelnut Fig Muffins

Total Time Taken: 1 hour
Yield: 12 Servings
Ingredients:

- ¼ cup canola oil
- ½ cup all-purpose flour
- ½ cup light brown sugar
- ½ teaspoon salt
- 1 cup ground hazelnuts
- 1 teaspoon baking powder
- 12 fresh figs
- 4 eggs

Directions:

1. Mix the hazelnuts, flour, salt and baking powder in a container.
2. Mix the eggs and sugar in a container until pale and light. Put in the oil and mix thoroughly.
3. Fold in the flour and hazelnut mixture then pour the batter in a muffin tin covered with muffin papers.
4. Top each muffin with a fig and preheat your oven and bake at 350F for about twenty minutes or until it rises significantly and seems golden.

These muffins taste best chilled.

Nutritional Content of One Serving:

Calories: 190 Fat: 10.0g Protein: 4.0g Carbohydrates: 23.4g

Healthy Chocolate Muffins

Total Time Taken: 1 hour
Yield: 12 Servings
Ingredients:

- ¼ teaspoon salt
- ½ cup cocoa powder
- ½ cup low fat milk
- ½ cup maple syrup
- 1 ½ cups whole wheat flour
- 1 ½ teaspoons baking powder
- 1 cup plain yogurt
- 1 egg
- 1 teaspoon vanilla extract

Directions:

1. Mix the flour, baking powder, salt and cocoa powder in a container.
2. Put in the remaining ingredients and stir for a few seconds to mix.
3. Spoon the batter in a muffin tin covered with muffin papers and preheat your oven and bake at 350F for about twenty minutes or until a toothpick inserted into them comes out dry.
4. Let cool in the pan before you serve.

Nutritional Content of One Serving:
Calories: 125 Fat: 1.4g Protein: 4.2g Carbohydrates: 25.0g

Honey Cardamom Cupcakes

Total Time Taken: 1 ½ hours
Yield: 12 Servings
Ingredients:

Cupcakes:

- ½ cup butter, softened
- ½ cup honey
- ½ teaspoon salt
- 1 ½ cups all-purpose flour
- 1 ½ teaspoons baking powder
- 1 teaspoon ground cardamom
- 1 teaspoon vanilla extract
- 1/3 cup milk
- 2 eggs
- 2 tablespoons dark brown sugar

Frosting:

- ¼ cup honey
- 1 cup butter, softened

- 1 teaspoon vanilla extract
- 2 cups powdered sugar

Directions:

1. To make the cupcakes, combine the butter, honey and sugar in a container until fluffy and pale. Put in the vanilla and eggs and mix thoroughly.
2. Fold in the flour, salt, baking powder and cardamom, alternating them with milk.
3. Spoon the batter in a muffin tin covered with muffin papers.
4. Pre-heat the oven and bake at 350F for about twenty minutes or until a golden-brown colour is achieved.
5. Let them cool in the pan.
6. To make the frosting, combine the butter and sugar in a container for about five to seven minutes until fluffy and pale. Stir in the vanilla and mix thoroughly.
7. Spoon the frosting into a pastry and top each cupcake with it.
8. Sprinkle the frosted cupcakes with honey.

Nutritional Content of One Serving:

Calories: 425 Fat: 24.1g Protein: 3.1g Carbohydrates: 51.7g

Nutella Peanut Butter Cupcakes

Total Time Taken: 1 ½ hours
Yield: 12 Servings
Ingredients:

Cupcakes:

- ¼ cup butter, softened
- ¼ teaspoon salt
- ½ cup buttermilk
- ½ cup smooth peanut butter
- ¾ cup light brown sugar
- 1 ½ cups all-purpose flour
- 1 ½ teaspoons baking powder
- 1 teaspoon vanilla extract
- 2 eggs

Frosting:

- 1 cup Nutella

Directions:

1. To make the cupcakes, combine the peanut butter, butter, sugar and vanilla in a container until creamy.
2. Put in the eggs and buttermilk and mix thoroughly.
3. Fold in the remaining ingredients then spoon the batter in a muffin tin covered with muffin papers.
4. Pre-heat the oven and bake at 350F for about twenty minutes or until it rises significantly and starts to appear golden-brown.
5. When chilled, top with Nutella and serve fresh.

Nutritional Content of One Serving:

Calories: 221 Fat: 11.2g Protein: 5.8g Carbohydrates: 25.7g

Nutella Stuffed Strawberry Muffins

Total Time Taken: 1 hour
Yield: 12 Servings
Ingredients:

- ¼ teaspoon salt
- ½ cup canola oil
- ½ cup Nutella
- ¾ cup milk
- 1 cup strawberries, sliced
- 1 cup white sugar
- 1 teaspoon vanilla extract
- 2 cups all-purpose flour
- 2 eggs
- 2 teaspoons baking powder

Directions:

1. Mix the eggs and sugar in a container until fluffy and pale.
2. Put in the vanilla and oil and mix thoroughly.
3. Stir in the milk then put in the flour, salt and baking powder and mix using a spatula.
4. Spoon half of the batter evenly in a muffin tin covered with muffin papers.
5. Top with a dollop of Nutella then spoon the rest of the batter over the Nutella.
6. Pre-heat the oven and bake at 350F for about twenty minutes or until fluffy and golden brown.
7. Let cool in the pan before you serve.

Nutritional Content of One Serving:
Calories: 259 Fat: 11.4g Protein: 3.8g Carbohydrates: 36.5g

Nutty Chocolate Chip Muffins

Total Time Taken: 1 hour
Yield: 12 Servings
Ingredients:

- 2 eggs
- 1 teaspoon vanilla extract
- 1 teaspoon baking powder
- 1 cup white sugar
- 1 cup walnuts, chopped
- 1 cup buttermilk
- 1 ½ cups all-purpose flour
- ½ teaspoon baking soda
- ½ cup dark chocolate chips
- ½ cup cocoa powder
- ¼ teaspoon salt

- ¼ cup canola oil

Directions:

1. Mix the flour, cocoa powder, sugar, baking soda, baking powder and salt in a container.
2. Put in the eggs, oil, vanilla and buttermilk and stir for a few seconds to mix.
3. Fold in the walnuts and chocolate chips then pour the batter in a muffin tin lined using muffin papers of your choice.
4. Pre-heat the oven and bake at 350F for about twenty minutes or until a toothpick inserted into them comes out dry.

These muffins taste best chilled.

Nutritional Content of One Serving:

Calories: 275 Fat: 13.6g Protein: 6.7g Carbohydrates: 36.2g

Nutty Double Chocolate Muffins

Total Time Taken: 1 hour
Yield: 12 Servings
Ingredients:

- ¼ cup canola oil
- ¼ cup cocoa powder
- ½ cup ground hazelnuts
- ½ teaspoon salt
- 1 1/2 cup all-purpose flour
- 1 cup dark chocolate chips
- 1 cup milk
- 1 cup white sugar
- 1 egg
- 1 teaspoon baking powder
- 1 teaspoon vanilla extract

Directions:

1. Mix the flour, cocoa powder, ground hazelnuts, salt, baking powder and sugar in a container.
2. Put in the egg, canola oil, milk and vanilla and stir for a few seconds to mix.
3. Fold in the chocolate chips then spoon the batter in a muffin tin covered with muffin papers.
4. Preheat your oven and bake the muffins at 350F for about twenty minutes or until a toothpick inserted into them comes out dry.

These muffins taste best chilled.

Nutritional Content of One Serving:

Calories: 247 Fat: 10.3g Protein: 4.2g Carbohydrates: 38.0g

Oatmeal Carrot Muffins

Total Time Taken: 1 hour
Yield: 12 Servings
Ingredients:

- 2 eggs

- 2 cups grated carrots
- 1 teaspoon baking powder
- 1 cup rolled oats
- 1 cup buttermilk
- 1 cup all-purpose flour
- ½ teaspoon ground ginger
- ½ teaspoon cinnamon powder
- ½ teaspoon baking soda
- ½ cup light brown sugar
- ½ cup crushed pineapple
- ½ cup canola oil
- ¼ teaspoon salt

Directions:

1. Mix the oats, flour, baking soda, baking powder, salt, cinnamon, ginger and sugar in a container.
2. Stir in the eggs, oil and buttermilk and stir for a few seconds to mix.
3. Fold in the carrots and pineapple then spoon the batter in a muffin tin covered with muffin papers.
4. Preheat your oven and bake the muffins at 350F for about twenty minutes or until it rises significantly and starts to appear golden-brown.

These muffins taste best chilled.

Nutritional Content of One Serving:

Calories: 197 Fat: 10.5g Protein: 3.8g Carbohydrates: 22.5g

Oatmeal Cranberry Muffins

Total Time Taken: 1 hour
Yield: 12 Servings
Ingredients:

- ¼ cup candied orange peel, diced
- ¼ cup light brown sugar
- ¼ cup milk
- ¼ cup olive oil
- ¼ teaspoon salt
- 1 cup all-purpose flour
- 1 cup fresh cranberries
- 1 cup rolled oats
- 1 teaspoon vanilla extract
- 2 bananas, mashed
- 2 eggs
- 2 tablespoons ground flaxseeds
- 2 teaspoons baking powder

Directions:

1. Mix the bananas, eggs, milk, olive oil, sugar and vanilla in a container.
2. Fold in the flour, flaxseeds, oats, baking powder and salt then put in the cranberries and orange peel.
3. Spoon the batter in a muffin tin covered with muffin papers.
4. Pre-heat the oven and bake at 350F for about twenty minutes or until it rises completely and is aromatic.
5. Let cool in the pan before you serve.

Nutritional Content of One Serving:

Calories: 157 Fat: 6.0g Protein: 3.5g Carbohydrates: 22.4g

Orange Almond Muffins

Total Time Taken: 1 ½ hours
Yield: 12 Servings

Ingredients:

- ½ teaspoon salt
- 1 cup white sugar
- 1 teaspoon baking powder
- 1 teaspoon vanilla extract
- 2 cups almond flour
- 2 small oranges
- 6 eggs

Directions:

1. Put the oranges in a saucepan and cover them with water. Boil the oranges for about half an hour until softened. Drain the oranges well and place them in a blender. Pulse until the desired smoothness is achieved.
2. Mix the eggs and sugar in a container until fluffy and pale.
3. Stir in the oranges then fold in the almond flour, baking powder and salt.
4. Spoon the batter in a muffin tin covered with muffin papers.
5. Preheat your oven and bake the muffins at 350F for about twenty minutes or until it rises significantly and starts to appear golden-brown.
6. Let the muffins cool to room temperature before you serve.

Nutritional Content of One Serving:

Calories: 130 Fat: 4.5g Protein: 3.9g Carbohydrates: 20.0g

Orange Glazed Cupcakes

Total Time Taken: 1 ½ hours
Yield: 12 Servings
Ingredients:

Cupcakes:

- ¼ cup candied ginger, chopped
- ¼ cup molasses
- ¼ teaspoon salt
- ½ cup butter, softened

- ½ teaspoon baking powder
- ½ teaspoon ground cloves
- ½ teaspoon ground ginger
- 1 cup light brown sugar
- 1 cup sour cream
- 1 tablespoon orange zest
- 1 teaspoon baking soda
- 1 teaspoon cinnamon powder
- 1 teaspoon grated ginger
- 2 cups all-purpose flour
- 2 eggs

Glaze:

- 1 cup powdered sugar
- 1 tablespoon orange juice
- 1 teaspoon vanilla extract

Directions:

1. To make the cupcakes, combine the butter, molasses and sugar in a container until creamy and pale.
2. Put in the sour cream, orange zest, ginger and eggs and mix thoroughly.
3. Fold in the flour, salt, baking soda, baking powder, cinnamon, ginger and cloves.
4. Fold in the ginger and mix using a spatula.
5. Spoon the batter in a muffin tin coated with baking muffin papers.
6. Pre-heat the oven and bake at 350F for about twenty minutes or until it rises significantly and becomes aromatic.
7. Let them cool down in the pan.
8. For the glaze, combine all the ingredients in a container.
9. Sprinkle the glaze over the cupcakes and serve them fresh.

Nutritional Content of One Serving:

Calories: 304 Fat: 12.7g Protein: 3.8g Carbohydrates: 44.6g

Orange Iced Cupcakes

Total Time Taken: 1 ¼ hours
Yield: 12 Servings

Ingredients:

- ¼ cup candied orange peel, diced
- ½ cup butter, softened
- ½ cup buttermilk
- ½ teaspoon salt
- ¾ cup white sugar
- 1 ½ teaspoons baking powder
- 1 ¾ cups all-purpose flour

- 1 teaspoon vanilla extract
- 3 eggs

Frosting:

- 1 ½ cups powdered sugar
- 1 tablespoon butter, melted
- 1 tablespoon orange juice
- 1 teaspoon orange zest

Directions:

1. To make the cupcakes, combine the butter and sugar in a container until fluffy and pale.
2. Put in the eggs and mix thoroughly then mix in the vanilla and buttermilk.
3. Fold in the flour, baking powder, salt and orange peel then spoon the batter in a muffin tin covered with muffin papers.
4. Pre-heat the oven and bake at 350F for about twenty minutes or until a toothpick inserted into them comes out dry. Let them cool in the pan.
5. For the glaze, combine all the ingredients in a container and mix thoroughly.
6. Sprinkle each cupcake with frosting.

Nutritional Content of One Serving:
Calories: 272 Fat: 10.0g Protein: 3.7g Carbohydrates: 42.9g

Orange Olive Oil Muffins

Total Time Taken: 1 hour
Yield: 12 Servings
Ingredients:

- ¼ cup olive oil
- ¼ teaspoon salt
- ½ cup fresh orange juice
- ½ cup sliced almonds
- 1 cup all-purpose flour
- 1 cup almond flour
- 1 cup white sugar
- 1 tablespoon orange zest
- 1 teaspoon baking powder
- 1 teaspoon vanilla extract
- 4 eggs

Directions:

1. Mix the eggs and sugar in a container until fluffy and pale.
2. Put in the orange juice, oil, vanilla and orange zest and mix thoroughly.
3. Fold in the flours, salt and baking powder then spoon the batter in a muffin tin coated with baking muffin papers.
4. Top each muffin with sliced almonds and preheat your oven and bake at 350F for about twenty minutes or until it rises significantly and starts to appear golden-brown.

These muffins taste best chilled.

Nutritional Content of One Serving:
Calories: 200 Fat: 8.9g Protein: 4.4g Carbohydrates: 27.5g

Orange Pecan Muffins

Total Time Taken: 1 ¼ hours
Yield: 12 Servings

Ingredients:

- ¼ cup fresh orange juice
- ¼ teaspoon cinnamon
- ¼ teaspoon salt
- ½ cup dried cranberries
- ½ cup milk
- ½ cup white sugar
- 1 ½ teaspoons baking powder
- 1 ¾ cups all-purpose flour
- 1 cup pecans, chopped
- 1 tablespoon orange zest
- 2 eggs
- 6 tablespoons butter, melted

Directions:

1. Mix the flour, salt, baking powder, sugar and cinnamon in a container.
2. Put in the eggs, butter, milk, orange juice and orange zest and stir for a few seconds to mix.
3. Fold in the pecans and cranberries then spoon the batter in a muffin tin coated with baking muffin papers.
4. Preheat your oven and bake the muffins at 350F for about twenty minutes or until it rises significantly and seems golden.
5. *Let cool down before you serve.*

Nutritional Content of One Serving:
Calories: 178 Fat: 7.7g Protein: 3.4g Carbohydrates: 24.4g

Orange Poppy Seed Muffins

Total Time Taken: 1 ½ hours
Yield: 12 Servings

Ingredients:

- ½ cup coconut oil
- ½ cup whole wheat flour
- ½ teaspoon salt
- 1 ½ teaspoon baking powder
- 1 cup all-purpose flour
- 1 orange, washed

- 1 teaspoon vanilla extract
- 2 tablespoons poppy seed
- 3 eggs

Directions:

1. Put the orange in a saucepan and cover it with water. Cook until softened then drain and place the orange in a blender.
2. Put in the coconut oil, eggs and vanilla and blend until the desired smoothness is achieved.
3. Stir in the flours, salt, baking powder and poppy seed and mix using a spatula.
4. Spoon the batter in a muffin tin covered with muffin papers and preheat your oven and bake at 350F for about twenty minutes or until it rises significantly and seems golden.

These muffins taste best chilled.

Nutritional Content of One Serving:

Calories: 168 Fat: 11.0g Protein: 3.4g Carbohydrates: 14.5g

Orange Soda Cupcakes

Total Time Taken: 1 ½ cups
Yield: 12 Servings
Ingredients:

Cupcakes:

- ¼ cup vegetable oil
- ¼ teaspoon salt
- ½ cup butter, softened
- ½ cup white sugar 3 egg whites
- 1 ¼ cups orange soda
- 1 ½ cups all-purpose flour
- 1 ½ teaspoons baking powder
- 1 cup cream cheese
- 1 teaspoon orange zest **Frosting:**
- 1 teaspoon vanilla extract
- 2 cups powdered sugar
- 2 tablespoons heavy cream

Directions:

1. To make the cupcakes, combine the egg whites, oil, orange soda and orange zest in a container.
2. Put in the remaining ingredients then spoon the batter in a muffin tin covered with muffin papers.
3. Pre-heat the oven and bake at 350F for about twenty minutes or until a toothpick inserted into them comes out dry.
4. Let cool in the pan.
5. To make the frosting, combine the butter and cream cheese in a container until fluffy.
6. Put in the sugar and mix for five minutes on high speed.
7. Stir in the cream and vanilla and mix for 1 additional minute.
8. Pipe the frosting over each cupcake and serve them fresh.

Nutritional Content of One Serving:
Calories: 368 Fat: 20.1g Protein: 4.1g Carbohydrates: 44.4g

Orange Yogurt Muffins

Total Time Taken: 1 hour
Yield: 12 Servings
Ingredients:

- ¼ cup candied orange peel, chopped
- ½ cup canola oil
- ½ teaspoon salt
- 1 cup plain yogurt
- 1 egg
- 1 orange, zested and juice
- 2 cups all-purpose flour
- 2 teaspoons baking powder

Directions:

1. Mix the flour, baking powder and salt in a container.
2. Put in the yogurt, orange zest, orange juice, oil and egg and mix thoroughly.
3. Fold in the orange peel then spoon the batter in a muffin tin lined using muffin papers of your choice.
4. Pre-heat the oven and bake at 350F for about twenty minutes or until it rises significantly and starts to appear golden-brown.

These muffins taste best chilled.

Nutritional Content of One Serving:
Calories: 186 Fat: 9.9g Protein: 3.9g Carbohydrates: 20.1g

Oreo Cream Cupcakes

Total Time Taken: 1 ½ hours
Yield: 12 Servings
Ingredients:

Cupcakes:

- ¼ teaspoon salt
- 1 cup butter, softened
- 1 cup buttermilk
- 1 cup white sugar
- 1 tablespoon vanilla extract
- 2 cups all-purpose flour
- 2 eggs
- 2 teaspoons baking powder
- 6 Oreo cookies, crushed

Topping:

- 2 cups heavy cream, whipped

- 6 Oreo cookies, chopped

Directions:

1. To make the cupcakes, combine the flour, salt, baking powder and sugar in a container.
2. Put in the butter and stir until grainy.
3. In a small container, mix the eggs, buttermilk and vanilla. Pour this mixture progressively over the flour and mix for a minute on high speed.
4. Spoon the batter in a muffin tin covered with muffin papers.
5. Pre-heat the oven and bake at 350F for about twenty minutes or until it rises significantly and starts to appear golden-brown.
6. Let cool down before you serve.

Nutritional Content of One Serving:

Calories: 412 Fat: 25.8g Protein: 4.9g Carbohydrates: 41.9g

Passionfruit Cupcakes

Total Time Taken: 1 ½ hours
Yield: 12 Servings
Ingredients:

Cupcakes:

- ¼ cup passionfruit juice
- ½ cup butter, softened
- ½ cup milk
- ½ cup white sugar
- ½ teaspoon salt
- 1 ½ teaspoons baking powder
- 1 13/4 cups all-purpose flour
- 1 teaspoon vanilla extract
- 2 eggs

Frosting:

- 1 cup butter, softened
- 2 cups powdered sugar
- 2 tablespoons passionfruit juice

Directions:

1. To make the cupcakes, combine the butter and sugar in a container until pale and light.
2. Put in the eggs and mix thoroughly then mix in the vanilla, passionfruit juice and milk.
3. Fold in the flour, salt and baking powder then spoon the batter in a muffin tin covered with muffin papers.
4. Pre-heat the oven and bake at 350F for about twenty minutes or until a golden-brown colour is achieved.
5. Let the cupcakes cool down.
6. To make the frosting, combine the butter and sugar in a container for five minutes until pale.
7. Stir in the passionfruit juice and mix thoroughly.
8. Top each cupcake with the frosting and serve fresh.

Nutritional Content of One Serving:
Calories: 494 Fat: 24.4g Protein: 6.1g Carbohydrates: 63.8g

Peach and Cream Muffins

Total Time Taken: 1 hour
Yield: 12 Servings
Ingredients:

- ¼ teaspoon salt
- ½ cup white sugar
- 1 cup butter, melted
- 1 cup sour cream
- 1 teaspoon vanilla extract
- 2 cups all-purpose flour
- 2 peaches, pitted and diced
- 2 teaspoons baking powder

Directions:

1. Mix the butter, sour cream, sugar and vanilla in a container until creamy.
2. Put in the flour, baking powder and salt then fold in the peaches.
3. Spoon the batter in a muffin tin covered with muffin papers and preheat your oven and bake at 350F for about twenty minutes or until a golden-brown colour is achieved and it rises significantly.

These muffins taste best chilled.

Nutritional Content of One Serving:
Calories: 292 Fat: 19.6g Protein: 3.1g Carbohydrates: 27.1g

Peachy Muffins

Total Time Taken: 1 hour
Yield: 12 Servings
Ingredients:

- ½ cup canola oil
- ½ cup plain yogurt
- ½ cup whole wheat flour
- ½ teaspoon salt
- ¾ cup white sugar
- 1 cup all-purpose flour
- 1 teaspoon baking soda
- 2 eggs
- 2 peaches, pitted and diced
- 2 tablespoons chia seeds

Directions:

1. Mix the flours, salt, chia seeds and baking soda in a container.
2. Mix the oil, sugar and eggs in another container and whip until volume increases to twice what it was.

3. Put in the yogurt then mix in the flour. Fold in the peaches.
4. Spoon the batter in a muffin tin covered with muffin papers.
5. Preheat your oven and bake the muffins at 350F for about twenty minutes or until it rises significantly and starts to appear golden-brown.

These muffins taste best chilled.

Nutritional Content of One Serving:

Calories: 219 Fat: 10.9g Protein: 3.8g Carbohydrates: 26.9g

Peanut Butter Banana Cupcakes

Total Time Taken: 1 ½ hours
Yield: 12 Servings
Ingredients:

Cupcakes:

- ¼ teaspoon salt
- ½ cup canola oil
- ½ cup milk
- 1 ¾ cups all-purpose flour
- 1 egg
- 1 teaspoon baking soda
- 1 teaspoon vanilla extract
- 2 bananas, mashed

Frosting:

- ½ cup smooth peanut butter
- 1 cup cream cheese
- 1 cup powdered sugar

Directions:

1. To make the cupcakes, combine the bananas, canola oil, milk, egg and vanilla.
2. Stir in the flour, salt and baking soda then spoon the batter in a muffin tin covered with muffin papers.
3. Pre-heat the oven and bake at 350F for about twenty minutes or until it rises significantly and starts to appear golden-brown.
4. To make the frosting, combine all the ingredients in a container until creamy and fluffy.
5. Apply the frosting on top of each cupcake and serve them fresh.

Nutritional Content of One Serving:

Calories: 345 Fat: 22.1g Protein: 7.0g Carbohydrates: 31.5g

Pear and Ginger Muffins

Total Time Taken: 1 hour
Yield: 12 Servings
Ingredients:

- ¼ teaspoon salt
- ½ cup buttermilk
- ½ cup canola oil

- ½ cup dark chocolate chips
- ½ cup light brown sugar
- 1 ½ cups all-purpose flour
- 1 teaspoon baking soda
- 1 teaspoon grated ginger
- 1 teaspoon vanilla extract
- 2 eggs
- 2 pears, cored and diced

Directions:

1. Mix the eggs and sugar in a container until fluffy and pale. Stir in the oil and mix thoroughly then put in the buttermilk and mix thoroughly.
2. Stir in the vanilla and ginger then fold in the flour, salt and baking powder.
3. Put in the pears and dark chocolate and stir lightly using a spatula.
4. Spoon the batter in a muffin tin covered with muffin papers and preheat your oven and bake at 350F for about twenty minutes or until it rises significantly and starts to appear golden-brown.

These muffins taste best chilled.

Nutritional Content of One Serving:

Calories: 220 Fat: 11.4g Protein: 3.4g Carbohydrates: 27.2g

Pecan Pie Muffins

Total Time Taken: 1 hour
Yield: 10 Servings
Ingredients:

- 2 eggs
- 1 teaspoon vanilla extract
- 1 cup light brown sugar
- 1 cup butter, melted
- 1 ½ cups pecans, chopped
- ½ cup all-purpose flour
- ¼ teaspoon salt

Directions:

1. Mix the eggs and sugar in a container until fluffy and volume increases to twice what it was.
2. Put in the vanilla and melted butter and mix thoroughly.
3. Fold in the flour, pecans and salt then spoon the batter in a muffin tin covered with muffin papers.
4. Pre-heat the oven and bake at 350F for about twenty minutes or until a golden-brown colour is achieved.

These muffins taste best chilled.

Nutritional Content of One Serving:

Calories: 264 Fat: 20.3g Protein: 2.1g Carbohydrates: 19.3g

Persimmon Muffins

Total Time Taken: 1 hour
Yield: 12 Servings
Ingredients:

- ½ cup butter, melted
- ½ cup whole wheat flour
- ½ teaspoon cinnamon powder
- ½ teaspoon ground ginger
- ½ teaspoon salt
- ¾ cup buttermilk
- 1 ½ cups all-purpose flour
- 1 teaspoon vanilla extract
- 2 eggs
- 2 persimmon fruits, diced
- 2 teaspoons baking powder

Directions:

1. Mix the flours, salt, baking powder, ginger and cinnamon in a container.
2. Stir in the eggs, butter, buttermilk and vanilla and stir for a few seconds to mix.
3. Fold in the persimmon then spoon the batter in a muffin tin covered with muffin papers.
4. Pre-heat the oven and bake at 350F for about twenty minutes or until it rises significantly and starts to appear golden-brown.
5. Serve the muffins chilled or store them in an airtight container for maximum four days.

Nutritional Content of One Serving:

Calories: 182 Fat: 8.7g Protein: 3.8g Carbohydrates: 22.4g

Pink Coconut Cupcakes

Total Time Taken: 1 ½ hours
Yield: 12 Servings
Ingredients:

Cupcakes:

- ½ cup butter, softened
- ½ cup shredded coconut
- ½ cup white sugar
- ½ teaspoon salt
- 1 ½ cups all-purpose flour
- 1 teaspoon baking powder
- 1 teaspoon vanilla extract
- 2 eggs
- 2/3 cup whole milk

Frosting:

- ½ teaspoon pink food coloring
- 1 cup butter, softened
- 2 cups powdered sugar
- 2 tablespoons heavy cream

Directions:

1. To make the cupcakes, combine the butter, sugar and vanilla in a container until fluffy and pale.
2. Put in the eggs and mix thoroughly then fold in the flour, salt, baking powder and coconut, alternating it with milk.
3. Spoon the batter in a muffin tin covered with muffin papers and preheat your oven and bake at 350F for about twenty minutes or until a golden-brown colour is achieved and it rises significantly.
4. Let the cupcakes cool down.
5. To make the frosting, combine the butter and sugar in a container until fluffy and pale.
6. Put in the cream and food colouring and continue mixing a few additional minutes until airy.
7. Spoon the frosting on top of each cupcake before you serve.

Nutritional Content of One Serving:
Calories: 410 Fat:26.4g Protein: 3.4g Carbohydrates: 41.7g

Pink Lemonade Cupcakes

Total Time Taken: 1 ½ hours
Yield: 12 Servings
Ingredients:
Cupcakes:

- ¼ teaspoon salt
- ½ cup milk
- ¾ cup butter, softened
- 1 cup white sugar
- 1 drop red food coloring
- 1 egg white
- 1 tablespoon lemon zest
- 1 teaspoon vanilla extract
- 2 ½ cups all-purpose flour
- 2 eggs
- 2 tablespoons lemon juice
- 2 teaspoons baking powder

Frosting:

- 1 cup butter
- 1 drop red food coloring
- 2 cups powdered sugar

Directions:

1. To make the cupcakes, combine the butter and sugar in a container until fluffy and pale.
2. Put in the eggs and egg white and mix thoroughly.

183

3. Stir in the vanilla, lemon juice, lemon zest, milk and food colouring and mix thoroughly.

4. Put in the dry ingredients and fold them in using a spatula.

5. Spoon the batter in a muffin tin covered with muffin papers.

6. Pre-heat the oven and bake at 350F for about twenty minutes or until a golden-brown colour is achieved and it rises significantly.

7. Let cool in the pan.

8. To make the frosting, combine the butter in a container until fluffy. Put in the sugar and continue mixing for a few minutes on high speed.

9. Put in the food colouring then pipe the frosting over each cupcake.

The cupcakes taste best chilled.

Nutritional Content of One Serving:

Calories: 442 Fat: 24.1g Protein: 3.9g Carbohydrates: 54.6g

Pink Velvet Cupcakes

Total Time Taken: 1 ½ hours
Yield: 12 Servings
Ingredients:

Cupcakes:

- ¼ teaspoon red food coloring
- ½ cup sour cream
- ½ cup white sugar
- ½ teaspoon salt
- 1 ½ teaspoon baking powder
- 1 2/3 cups all-purpose flour
- 1 egg
- 1 teaspoon vanilla extract

Frosting:

- 1 cup butter, softened
- 1 teaspoon vanilla extract
- 2 cups powdered sugar

Directions:

1. To make the cupcakes, combine the egg and sugar until pale. Put in the vanilla and mix thoroughly then mix in the sour cream and food coloring.

2. Stir in the remaining ingredients and stir for a few seconds to mix.

3. Spoon the batter in 12 muffin cups covered with muffin papers.

4. Preheat your oven and bake the cupcakes at 350F for about twenty minutes or until the cupcake pass the toothpick test.

5. Let the cupcakes cool down.

6. To make the frosting, combine the butter until pale. Put in the sugar and stir thoroughly until blended.

7. Stir in the vanilla and mix thoroughly then spoon the buttercream in a pastry bag and pipe on each cupcake.

Nutritional Content of One Serving:

Calories: 336 Fat: 17.9g Protein: 2.7g Carbohydrates: 42.3g

Plum Whole Wheat Muffins

Total Time Taken: 1 hour
Yield: 12 Servings
Ingredients:

- ¼ cup all-purpose flour
- ¼ cup canola oil
- ½ cup buttermilk
- ½ teaspoon salt
- 1 ½ cups whole wheat flour
- 1 tablespoon chia seeds
- 1 teaspoon vanilla extract
- 2 eggs
- 2 teaspoons baking powder
- 4 plums, pitted and diced

Directions:

1. Mix the flours, baking powder, salt and chia seeds in a container.
2. Put in the remaining ingredients and stir for a few seconds to mix using a spatula.
3. Spoon the batter in a muffin tin covered with muffin papers.
4. Preheat your oven and bake the muffins at 350F for about twenty minutes or until it rises significantly and seems golden.

These muffins taste best chilled.

Nutritional Content of One Serving:

Calories: 142 Fat: 6.4g Protein: 3.8g Carbohydrates: 17.4g

Pumpkin Apple Muffins

Total Time Taken: 1 ¼ hours
Yield: 12 Servings
Ingredients:

- 2 red apples, cored and diced
- 2 eggs
- 1 teaspoon pumpkin pie spices
- 1 teaspoon baking soda
- 1 cup pumpkin puree
- 1 ½ cups whole wheat flour
- ½ teaspoon salt
- ½ teaspoon baking powder
- ½ cup light brown sugar
- ½ cup canola oil
- ½ cup all-purpose flour

- ¼ cup milk

Directions:

1. Mix the flours, baking soda, baking powder, salt and spices in a container.
2. Put in the eggs, pumpkin puree, milk, oil and sugar and stir for a few seconds to mix.
3. Fold in the apples then spoon the batter in a muffin tin covered with muffin papers.
4. Pre-heat the oven and bake at 350F for about twenty minutes or until it rises significantly and starts to appear golden-brown.

These muffins taste best chilled.

Nutritional Content of One Serving:

Calories: 215 Fat: 10.2g Protein: 3.6g Carbohydrates: 28.2g

Pumpkin Apple Streusel Muffins

Total Time Taken: 1 ¼ hours
Yield: 14 Servings
Ingredients:

Muffins:

- ¼ cup canola oil
- ¼ teaspoon salt
- ½ cup oat flour
- 1 ¼ cups pumpkin puree
- 1 cup white sugar
- 1 teaspoon baking powder
- 1 teaspoon baking soda
- 1 teaspoon pumpkin pie spices
- 2 apples, peeled and diced
- 2 cups all-purpose flour
- 2 eggs

Streusel:

- ¼ cup butter
- ¼ cup rolled oats
- ½ cup all-purpose flour
- 1 pinch salt
- 2 tablespoons dark brown sugar

Directions:

1. For the muffins, combine the flours, sugar, baking soda, baking powder, salt and spices in a container.
2. Put in the pumpkin puree, eggs, canola oil and apples and stir for a few seconds to mix.
3. Spoon the batter in a muffin tin covered with muffin papers.
4. Pre-heat the oven and bake at 350F for about twenty minutes or until it rises completely and is aromatic.
5. *Let cool down before you serve.*

Nutritional Content of One Serving:

Calories: 252 Fat: 8.5g Protein: 4.1g Carbohydrates: 41.5g

Pumpkin Chocolate Chip Muffins

Total Time Taken: 1 hour
Yield: 12 Servings
Ingredients:

- 2 eggs
- 1 teaspoon vanilla extract
- 1 teaspoon baking soda
- 1 cup pumpkin puree
- 1 ½ cups all-purpose flour
- ½ teaspoon ground star anise
- ½ teaspoon ground ginger
- ½ teaspoon cinnamon powder
- ½ cup oat flour
- ½ cup dark chocolate chips
- ¼ teaspoon salt
- ¼ cup canola oil

Directions:

1. Mix the pumpkin puree, oil, eggs and vanilla in a container and mix thoroughly.
2. Fold in the flours, salt, baking soda and spices.
3. Spoon the batter in a muffin tin covered with muffin papers.
4. Preheat your oven and bake the muffins at 350F for about twenty minutes or until it rises significantly and starts to appear golden-brown.

These muffins taste best chilled.

Nutritional Content of One Serving:

Calories: 155 Fat: 7.1g Protein: 3.6g Carbohydrates: 19.8g

Flourless Peanut Butter Cookies

Total Time Taken: 1 hour
Yield: 30 Servings
Ingredients:

- ½ teaspoon salt
- 1 cup light brown sugar
- 2 cups smooth peanut butter
- 2 eggs

Directions:

1. Combine all the ingredients in a container until the desired smoothness is achieved.
2. Drop spoonfuls of mixture on a baking sheet coated with baking paper.
3. Score the top of each cookie with a fork then preheat your oven and bake the cookies at 350F for about ten minutes.

4. *These cookies taste best chilled.*

Nutritional Content of One Serving:

Calories: 124 Fat: 9.0g Protein: 4.7g Carbohydrates: 8.1g

Four Ingredient Peanut Butter Cookies

Total Time Taken: 1 hour

Yield: 20 Servings

Ingredients:

- 1 cup rolled oats
- 1 cup smooth peanut butter
- 1 egg
- 2/3 cup light brown sugar

Directions:

1. Mix the peanut butter, egg and sugar in a container until creamy then put in the oats.
2. Drop spoonfuls of batter on a baking tray coated with baking paper.
3. Preheat your oven and bake the cookies at 350F for about fifteen minutes or until a golden-brown colour is achieved on the edges.
4. *These cookies taste best chilled.*

Nutritional Content of One Serving:

Calories: 113 Fat: 7.0g Protein: 4.1g Carbohydrates: 10.1g

Fresh Blueberry Cookies

Total Time Taken: 1 ½ hours

Yield: 30 Servings

Ingredients:

- ¼ cup whole milk
- ½ teaspoon baking soda
- ½ teaspoon salt
- 1 cup butter, softened
- 1 cup fresh blueberries
- 1 cup powdered sugar
- 1 egg
- 1 tablespoon lemon zest
- 1 teaspoon vanilla extract
- 2 cups all-purpose flour

Directions:

1. Mix the butter, vanilla and sugar in a container until fluffy and light.
2. Put in the egg, milk and lemon zest and mix thoroughly.
3. Stir in the flour, salt and baking soda and mix using a spatula then fold in the blueberries.
4. Drop spoonfuls of batter on a baking tray covered with parchment paper.

5. Pre-heat the oven and bake at 350F for about thirteen minutes or until a golden-brown colour is achieved on the edges.
6. *These cookies taste best chilled.*

Nutritional Content of One Serving:
Calories: 107 Fat: 6.5g Protein: 1.2g Carbohydrates: 11.2g

Fruity Cookies

Total Time Taken: 1 ½ hours
   Yield: 30 Servings
Ingredients:
- 2 tablespoons molasses
- 2 tablespoons golden syrup
- 1 egg
- ¼ cup milk
- 2 cups all-purpose flour
- ¼ teaspoon salt
- 1 teaspoon baking soda
- ½ cup sultanas
- ½ cup dried cranberries
- ½ cup raisins
- ½ cup dried apricots, chopped
- ¼ cup Grand Marnier
- 2/3 cup butter, softened
- 2/3 cup white sugar

Directions:
1. Mix the fruits with Grand Marnier in a container and allow to soak up for about half an hour.
2. Mix the butter, sugar, molasses and golden syrup in a container until pale.
3. Put in the egg and milk and mix thoroughly.
4. Put in the dry ingredients then fold in the fruits.
5. Drop spoonfuls of batter on a baking sheet coated with baking paper and preheat your oven and bake the cookies at 350F for fifteen minutes.
6. Let the cookies cool down before you serve.

Nutritional Content of One Serving:
Calories: 111 Fat: 4.4g Protein: 1.3g Carbohydrates: 15.7g

Fudgy Chocolate Cookies

Total Time Taken: 1 ¼ hours
   Yield: 30 Servings
Ingredients:
- ¼ teaspoon salt
- ½ cup butter

- ½ cup light brown sugar
- 1 ½ cups dark chocolate chips
- 1 teaspoon baking powder
- 1 teaspoon vanilla extract
- 2 eggs
- 2 tablespoons white sugar
- 2/3 cup all-purpose flour

Directions:

1. Melt the butter and chocolate in a heatproof container over a hot water bath.
2. Mix the eggs and sugars in a container until fluffy and pale.
3. Stir in the chocolate and mix using a spatula.
4. Fold in the flour, baking powder and salt then drop spoonfuls of batter in a baking sheet coated with baking paper.
5. Preheat your oven and bake the cookies at 350F for about thirteen minutes.
6. *These cookies taste best chilled.*

Nutritional Content of One Serving:

Calories: 82 Fat: 5.0g Protein: 1.1g Carbohydrates: 9.4g

German Chocolate Cookies

Total Time Taken: 1 ¼ hours
Yield: 30 Servings

Ingredients:

- ¼ cup cocoa powder
- ½ cup coconut flakes
- ½ cup dark chocolate chips
- ½ cup white sugar
- ½ teaspoon salt
- 1 cup butter, softened
- 1 cup light brown sugar
- 1 cup pecans, chopped
- 1 teaspoon baking soda
- 2 ¼ cups all-purpose flour
- 2 eggs

Directions:

1. Mix the butter and sugars in a container until pale and creamy.
2. Put in the eggs and mix thoroughly then fold in the flour, cocoa powder, baking soda and salt.
3. Fold in the chocolate chips, coconut flakes and pecans.
4. Drop spoonfuls of batter on baking trays coated with baking paper.
5. Preheat your oven and bake the cookies at 350F for about fifteen minutes or until risen.
6. *These cookies taste best chilled.*

Nutritional Content of One Serving:

Calories: 142 Fat: 7.9g Protein: 1.8g Carbohydrates: 17.2g

Ginger Almond Biscotti

Total Time Taken: 1 ¼ hours
 Yield: 20 Servings
Ingredients:

- ¼ teaspoon baking soda
- ½ cup blanched almonds
- ½ cup butter, softened
- ½ teaspoon salt
- ¾ cup white sugar
- 1 teaspoon baking powder
- 1 teaspoon ground ginger
- 1 teaspoon vanilla extract
- 2 cups all-purpose flour
- 2 eggs
- 2 tablespoons dark brown sugar
- 2 tablespoons molasses

Directions:

1. Mix the sugars, molasses, eggs and butter in a container until creamy.
2. Put in the vanilla then fold in the remaining ingredients.
3. Transfer the dough to a baking tray covered with parchment paper and shape it into a log.
4. Preheat your oven and bake the log at 350F for fifteen minutes or until a golden-brown colour is achieved on the edges.
5. When finished, let cool down slightly then cut the log into thin slices and place them back on the baking tray with the cut facing up.
6. Preheat your oven and bake the cookies at 350F for another ten to fifteen minutes.
7. Serve the biscotti chilled.

Nutritional Content of One Serving:
Calories: 145 Fat: 6.4g Protein: 2.4g Carbohydrates: 20.2g

Ginger Butter Cookies

Total Time Taken: 1 ¼ hours
 Yield: 20 Servings
Ingredients:

- ¼ teaspoon salt
- ½ cup butter, softened
- ½ teaspoon baking soda
- ½ teaspoon ground cardamom
- ¾ cup light brown sugar
- 1 ½ cups all-purpose flour

191

- 1 egg
- 1 teaspoon ground ginger
- 1 teaspoon vanilla extract

Directions:

1. Mix the butter and sugar until fluffy and pale. Put in the egg and vanilla and mix thoroughly.
2. Stir in the flour, ginger, cardamom, salt and baking soda.
3. Drop spoonfuls of batter on baking trays coated with baking paper.
4. Preheat your oven and bake the cookies at 350F for about fifteen minutes or until a golden-brown colour is achieved and crisp on the edges.
5. *These cookies taste best chilled.*

Nutritional Content of One Serving:

Calories: 100 Fat: 4.9g Protein: 1.3g Carbohydrates: 12.6g

Ginger Chocolate Oatmeal Cookies

Total Time Taken: 1 ¼ hours
Yield: 30 Servings

Ingredients:

- ¼ teaspoon salt
- ½ teaspoon baking soda
- ½ teaspoon cinnamon powder
- 1 cup all-purpose flour
- 1 cup light brown sugar
- 1 cup rolled oats
- 1 egg
- 1 teaspoon grated ginger
- 2 tablespoons cocoa powder
- 2/3 cup butter, softened

Directions:

1. Mix the butter and sugar until fluffy and creamy. Stir in the egg and mix thoroughly.
2. Put in the rest of the ingredients and mix using a spatula.
3. Drop spoonfuls of batter on a baking sheet coated with baking paper.
4. Pre-heat the oven and bake at 350F for fifteen minutes.
5. *These cookies taste best chilled.*

Nutritional Content of One Serving:

Calories: 83 Fat: 4.5g Protein: 1.1g Carbohydrates: 10.0g

Ginger Quinoa Cookies

Total Time Taken: 1 ¼ hours
Yield: 30 Servings

Ingredients:

- ¼ cup quinoa flakes

- ¼ cup quinoa flour
- ¼ teaspoon salt
- ½ cup almond flour
- ½ cup coconut oil, melted
- ½ cup light brown sugar
- ½ teaspoon baking soda
- ½ teaspoon cinnamon powder
- ½ teaspoon ground ginger
- 1 cup all-purpose flour
- 1 egg
- 2 tablespoons butter, softened
- 2 tablespoons molasses

Directions:

1. Mix the coconut oil and butter, molasses and sugar in a container until creamy and fluffy.
2. Put in the egg and mix thoroughly.
3. Stir in the remaining ingredients then drop spoonfuls of batter on a baking sheet coated with baking paper.
4. Preheat your oven and bake the cookies at 350F for about fifteen minutes or until a golden-brown colour is achieved on the edges.
5. These cookies taste best chilled.

Nutritional Content of One Serving:
Calories: 79 Fat: 5.0g Protein: 1.2g Carbohydrates: 7.6g

Gingerbread Cookies

Total Time Taken: 1 ¼ hours
Yield: 30 Servings

Ingredients:

- ¼ teaspoon salt
- ½ cup golden syrup
- ½ cup white sugar
- ½ teaspoon ground cardamom
- 1 cup butter, softened
- 1 egg
- 1 teaspoon baking soda
- 1 teaspoon cinnamon powder
- 1 teaspoon ground ginger
- 2 cups all-purpose flour
- 2 tablespoons dark molasses

Directions:

1. Mix the butter, golden syrup, sugar and molasses in a container until fluffy and pale.
2. Put in the egg and mix thoroughly then fold in the flour, spices, baking soda and salt.

3. Make small balls of dough and arrange them on a baking sheet coated with baking paper.
4. Pre-heat the oven and bake at 350F for fifteen minutes or until it is aromatic and appears golden.
5. *These cookies taste best chilled.*

Nutritional Content of One Serving:
Calories: 119 Fat: 6.4g Protein: 1.1g Carbohydrates: 15.0g

Gingerbread Cookies

Total Time Taken: 1 ¼ hours
Yield: 20 Servings
Ingredients:

- ¼ cup molasses
- ¼ teaspoon salt
- ½ cup butter, softened
- ½ cup ground almonds
- ½ cup light brown sugar
- ½ teaspoon baking soda
- ½ teaspoon cinnamon powder
- ½ teaspoon ground cloves
- ½ teaspoon ground ginger
- 1 egg
- 2 cups all-purpose flour

Directions:

1. Mix the butter, molasses and sugar in a container until pale and creamy.
2. Put in the egg and mix thoroughly then mix in the rest of the ingredients.
3. Make small balls of dough and place them on a baking tray coated with baking paper.
4. Preheat your oven and bake the cookies at 350F for about thirteen minutes or until aromatic, risen and golden.
5. *These cookies taste best chilled.*

Nutritional Content of One Serving:
Calories: 129 Fat: 6.2g Protein: 2.1g Carbohydrates: 16.8g

Gingersnap Cookies

Total Time Taken: 1 hour
Yield: 20 Servings
Ingredients:

- ¼ cup molasses
- ¼ teaspoon salt
- ½ teaspoon baking powder
- ½ teaspoon cinnamon powder
- ¾ cup canola oil
- ¾ cup light brown sugar

- 1 egg
- 1 teaspoon baking soda
- 1 teaspoon ground ginger
- 2 cups all-purpose flour

Directions:

1. Mix the oil, molasses and sugar in a container.
2. Put in the egg and stir until creamy and pale.
3. Fold in the remaining ingredients then form small balls and place them on baking trays coated with baking paper.
4. Preheat your oven and bake the cookies at 350F for about fifteen minutes or until crisp and fragrant.
5. *These cookies taste best chilled.*

Nutritional Content of One Serving:

Calories: 154 Fat: 8.5g Protein: 1.6g Carbohydrates: 18.1g

Made in the USA
Las Vegas, NV
19 December 2023

83174296R00109